2
3
49
18

CHANGE YOUR GAME

How To Achieve Your Full Potential As An Entrepreneur & Create The Life You Desire

BAIJU SOLANKI

Praise

'Baiju has simplified what it takes to develop your entrepreneurial mindset and make a game-changing impact. Explaining with great passion, he shows it's not just about the right mindset, it's about the strategy you have and the consistency of the actions you take. This is an inspired read that will get you to understand what is right for you and get you into action.'

— Daniel Priestley
Bestselling author of *Entrepreneur Revolution, Oversubscribed* and *24 Assets*

'Entrepreneurship is a game that should be played full out, and nobody reminds us of this better than Baiju! In *Change Your Game* he helps you tap into your purpose, gain clarity in your thinking and create real, lasting, positive change with an enterprise built on game-changing thinking. If you want to join the ranks of the new entrepreneurs making a real difference, read this book… and get in the game!'

— James Lavers
Founder, Lazy Coach, a digital publishing house for experts and entrepreneurs

'If you're interested in living your best life, this is the book for YOU. In the game of life the only constant is change, and Baiju helps you take apart your excuses and unleash your entrepreneurial spirit.'
— Julian 'The Ultrapreneur' Hall
  Founder of Ultra Education

'Baiju is a good man with a big heart and a passion for helping the start-up and entrepreneur. This book is a great resource for those with a dream, wanting to understand the steps needed both inside and out to make that entrepreneurial dream come true.'
— Deri Llewellyn-Davies
  Founder of BGI group and creator of Strategy on a Page

'There are many "self-help" books out there that focus on personal development and many more that teach you how to run a successful business. This, for me, is one of the only ones I have seen that has the perfect blend, in one book, to enable both personal and professional success as an entrepreneur. I guarantee there will be multiple lightbulb moments you'll get from learning how Baiju thinks. I highly recommend you put *Change Your Game* to the top of your reading list.'
— Will Polston
  Founder of Make It Happen and The Elite Network

'Baiju is someone who is clearly making waves for the great in the entrepreneurial community – well, that impact just got a major upgrade with his latest book, *Change Your Game*. If you're serious about reaching your full potential as an entrepreneur and making the impact you know you are destined for, then this is it: a practical nuts-and-bolts manual – thank you, Baiju.'

— Matt WL Noronha
    Mindset coach and sales trainer

'As an entrepreneur you're busy; I get it. If you're truly ready to change your game then here is your plan. This isn't about "more marketing" or "raising your prices"; it's about that deeper level of what will make YOU a game changer. Woman or man, newbie to your industry or long-time player, you HAVE to read this book. Simple, but life changing – follow the insights and make this your new bible. You'll want to read it again and again.'

— Yvette Taylor
    Creator of the Energy Alignment Method

'If you're looking to make a significant positive change in your life, this book could provide that spark of inspiration. Allow Baiju Solanki to help you unleash your entrepreneurial spirit!'

— Simon Hartley
    Founder of Be World Class, author and
    professional speaker

'The beauty of this book is that it explores one simple truth – we have an option this lifetime to be the best we can be. Baiju genuinely cares about whether we make the most of that opportunity and has presented us with a guidebook to help us on the way. His energy and passion come through in the pace of the narrative. It cajoles and invites you to look at yourself, make a decision, put in the hours and dig. Dig to find that part of you that can grow and flourish in your waking day. Dig to make the connections between how you think and what you do.'

— Sara Wilbourne
    Strategic communications specialist,
    international NGO sector

'In *Change Your Game*, Baiju teaches us to understand how to overcome our mindset, the importance of having a strategy, followed by taking action, focusing not only on the "how-to", but also sharing some amazing case studies of real people who have actually applied his methodology. Baiju writes with authority, compassion and insight. Essential reading for anyone embracing the world of business.'

— Warren Knight
    Creator of Think Digital First

'The truth is most people will not achieve the results this book makes possible – but if you are reading this book, you are not like most people. Baiju has a passion and commitment that impact the lives of people in his immediate line of sight and ripple into the wider world – a great book with insightful and pragmatic information.'

— Erkan Ali
    Creator and co-founder of BeCollaboration and Engage

'The Game of Life has two participants – spectators and players: choose one! Baiju Solanki illustrates so clearly that we are playing this game of life and we can choose how to have an impact. Whether you are starting a business, have got stuck in a rut, or are feeling dissatisfied where your life is heading, this book gives you the simple rules to follow to create the biggest impact. It resonates with me as I have always been a proponent of taking small, regular "steps to success" and he affirms that with direction on the mission, focus on the three pillars and consistency, everyone will attain their goal. Baiju is a big player in life, and reading this book will get you off the spectators' bench to START LIVING!'

— Gill Tiney
    Founder of Steps to Success and co-founder of BeCollaboration and Engage

'Wow, what a truly inspirational read for anyone looking to play a bigger game and get more from themselves in life and business. Baiju is a gifted author who understands the mechanics of how to live a rich and extraordinary life, and he has distilled his knowledge into some simple yet powerful steps that will truly help you *Change Your Game*.'
— Raghav Prakash
Peak Performance coach

'After reading this book it's clear that Baiju and I sing the same song and have the same attitude to life and business ... No excuses allowed ... Do whatever it takes. If you want continued success in your life, this book has everything you need to know.'
— Jean-Pierre De Villiers
Peak Performance coach

'This book is essential reading for all entrepreneurs. Baiju breaks down his experiences as an entrepreneur, coach and qualified psychologist to provide an indispensable actionable blueprint based on over two decades of application. A brilliant, well-researched, practical book and a manual for anyone who wants to elevate their current level of business success and effectiveness.'
— Aaron Love Yahaya
Speaker, investor and entrepreneur

'*Change Your Game* is a book that keeps things simple; at a time of overwhelming complexity and tremendous competition, the last thing you need is a book that compounds your frustration. *Change Your Game* is practical and straight to the point. It's not just a book; it will take your business and life to another level. I have been a student of Baiju Solanki for years and I know that his principles work. If you want to change your game, take action on the principles within it. I believe these are the same principles that have helped many entrepreneurs win the coveted prizes of success, freedom and profit. As I always say, "You don't have to be great to get started, but you have to get started to be great, so shut up and take action."'

— Action Jackson
Motivational speaker and entrepreneur

'Baiju gets it. This book will help you understand what it actually means to be an entrepreneur and live your life in a way that will set you up for success. No more winging it and making it up as you go along – this is your road map not only to winning the game, but to being a better entrepreneur along the way. Follow the advice in this book and you simply cannot fail.'

— Suraj Sodha
Entrepreneur and international speaker

'Baiju Solanki has distilled fifty-six core practices and techniques that are easy to understand and apply into a compelling playbook and narrative that are both pragmatic and emotionally energising.'
— Aftab Malhotra
Co-founder and chief growth officer of GrowthEnabler

'In *Change Your Game*, Baiju Solanki might just pull off the impossible. He deconstructs the mindset needed for success in the entrepreneurial arena. Now, many have written on this topic – that's not revolutionary – but where other volumes get bogged down in esoterica or business jargon, this book is clean, simple and easy to follow, while maintaining all of its power. We have all heard the old saw, "Success leaves clues", and with this work, you'll actually be able to follow those clues!'
— Manny Wolfe
Author of *The Tao of the Unbreakable Man* and creator of the 1000 Speakers Academy

'A great book that will do two things for you: 1) get you thinking deeper about where you could be heading, and 2) get you where you want to go a lot quicker. Highly recommended.'
— Simon Jordan
Brand consultant, author, speaker and environmentalist

'If ever you were uncertain about how to rise above your current circumstances and truly live the life you believe you were meant to live, then this book is for you! Simply written yet profoundly inspiring and practically delivered, Baiju's book helps you find the missing element and empower the dormant treasures within, to discover that we really are powerful beyond what we imagine or believe. I am happy to recommend this book, which I believe will change for the better the lives of those who read it!'

— Selwyn Cambridge
Founder of TEN Habitat, Caribbean
start-up incubator

R3THINK PRESS

First published in Great Britain 2018
by Rethink Press (www.rethinkpress.com)

Author photograph by Varinja Grewing
(www.varinjagrewing.com)

Contents

Foreword

I first met Baiju at an Ecademy event in 2007. As chairman I like to meet all my members where possible. I met a determined, strong, but somewhat confused individual: he knew what he wanted, but was not sure he knew how he was going to achieve it.

'Interesting character: charming, professional, intimate, but holds things back until he is ready to reveal them. I like that. Recommended, but not highly recommended until all is revealed. Clever, cunning, foxy – and good looking.' This is the testimonial I gave Baiju on LinkedIn back in November 2008.

Since then, over the years, I have seen him try, fail, persevere, and grow. One thing that is consistent is that he never gave up. This book is so typical of Baiju:

he is constantly playing the game and changing the rules. I will never forget the time Baiju organised a networking cricket match: we had many entrepreneurs playing and Baiju networked like the best of them. He is now seeing the fruits of his efforts, and of his open and generous approach.

My career has taken me from the corporate world, to running networks, to embracing new technology and advising FTSE 100 companies, so I know how relevant the tips in the book are to the world today. There is no secret source for success: you have to have a strong mind, you have to know where you are going, and you have to take action, consistently.

I have had massive success and massive failure, but, as Baiju confirms in this book, it's the people around you who keep you alive. Surround yourself with good people, believe in yourself and take decisive action. You may sometimes fail, but you will also succeed.

Baiju started off as an associate, but I am glad to say that he is now a friend, not only to me, but to also my wife Penny and my children Hannah, Ross and TJ.

Through his book, you now have the chance to benefit from Baiju's failures, successes, and the wisdom he has acquired along the way.

Thomas Power
Entrepreneur, investor, non-exec, speaker and author

Introduction

How many people do you know who are living the life they truly want? Are you? Do you wake up each day knowing that you will be doing exactly what you want to do? Being who you want to be? If not, why not?

I am only interested in excuses inasmuch as I can dismantle them to show you that what you want is possible. It took me thirty-seven years to start doing what I really wanted to do. Why did it take thirty-seven years? What was preventing me from making the choices?

If you'd asked me then, I would have said, 'Money, ability, lack of knowledge of what to do, responsibilities...' The usual life stuff. But truth be told, it was my mindset that was stopping me. The mindset I had by default was creating excuses, when actually what I lacked was belief in myself. I was using evidence around me to confirm that I couldn't do it, whatever 'it' may have been right there and then.

So what changed? I ran out of excuses, and I wish this had happened ten years earlier.

There were two occurrences that made me realise I had to make the change. The first happened while I was on a business trip to America, about to close one of the biggest deals in my employer's history. I got the deal; the commission was insane.

When I rang the office in London to tell my bosses the good news, they told me to take a few days off in New York on the company and enjoy myself. Was I happy? Of course I was – who wouldn't be? I was top dog, I earnt more in that deal than many do in six months, I was running my own team, and I had autonomy in my work.

After the call, I sat down on my hotel bed and congratulated myself. And then I said to myself, 'Is this it? Is this what my life is about – getting deals and making someone else money?'

I had never felt more empty. I knew I had to change things.

Six months later, I was attending the Tony Robbins UPW (Unleash the Power Within) four-day seminar in London. It was a proper up-beat rah-rah motivational seminar that made the attendees believe anything was possible. For me, it was perfect timing. I was already changing my mindset, going to events centred on starting a business and personal development, but UPW was on a different level. It confirmed everything I already knew, but had been afraid to admit:

- You are in charge of your own destiny

- You can choose to create a life you want

- You are the only person holding you back

- Money is a tool, not the answer to your problems

- You have to believe in yourself

- You need to surround yourself with the right people

- Now is the perfect time to start

And the most powerful learning of all was that there were no more excuses left.

Following those two life-changing moments, I took action and developed strategies to leave my job and start the business I wanted. On 14 October 2007, I handed my resignation letter in.

I want you to have the opportunity to live the life you desire by unleashing your entrepreneurial spirit. Over the years, many people have asked me how to do it. This book is your answer.

WHO IS THIS BOOK FOR?

This book is not just for people who want to start a business. Will it help these people? Yes, it will, but it is also for teachers, students, creative artists, singers, actors, healthcare workers, community leaders, politicians, middle managers, coaches, speakers, strategists, marketers, CEOs... the list goes on. In fact, it's for anyone who wants to love what they do and make a difference in the world.

This book is for all the people who ask themselves:

- Is this it?
- How can I do more in my life?
- How can I make more from the work I currently do?
- I love my job, but want to be able to do more?
- What can I give back to the world?
- Can I start my own business?
- How do I make an impact in my life?
- How do I make an impact in the world?

When you change your game, you release your authentic self and allow the world to see the true you. The system we live in doesn't make this easy for us; in fact, it actually works against us. It is therefore important that you take ownership and take charge of your life. The fifty-six top tips I share in this book will help you do just that.

Some people worry about the risk involved in making a change, but what is the risk really when failure is what you have now? The people you see loving what they do all took a risk. It didn't come easily. You only have one life, so make it count.

THE COMMON DENOMINATOR

I started writing this book in 2017, but it has actually been more than five years in the making. When I left my job and started my own business in 2007, it struck me how differently business owners and people who follow what they love think. They think in a way that empowers them, that allows them to deal with failure, and they have a resilience that enables them to keep going and focus on what they want to do.

This got me to wondering what it is entrepreneurs have that other people don't. Are they born with a particular spirit inside them, or do we all have it? In my book *I'm An Entrepreneur – Get Me Out Of Here*, I interviewed eleven entrepreneurs to find out what traits they have in common, and I found that they all think and feel the same way.

This confirmed something I have observed in the thousands of entrepreneurs I have met at hundreds of networking events over the last few years. There are two types of people, broadly speaking: those who do and those who wait. The ones who are doing have changed their mindset. They are making a game-changing impact, whereas the ones who are waiting are looking for some outside piece of knowledge or inner confidence before they make a start.

More than at any time in history, we have the resources, capacity, and environment to live the life we desire. We have the chance to unleash our entrepreneurial spirit to live a purposeful life and make a difference through the things we have control over. When we unleash that entrepreneurial spirit, we can change the game.

'What game?' you may ask. The game of your life; the game of your work; the game of your business.

Entrepreneurship is not just about starting a business; it's a way of thinking. To understand this, we need to go back to the etymology of the word 'entrepreneur'. The word comes from the French word *entreprendre*, meaning 'to undertake'. To be entrepreneurial is to commit to doing something, and I believe there is no greater undertaking than your life's purpose.

Approaching your life with an entrepreneurial mindset allows you to take control of it.

If we trace the word further back, it gets even better. The word 'entrepreneur' itself derives from the Sanskrit word *antarprerana*, which means self-motivation or inner motivation. The essence of this is that when we are driven from within, we are acting entrepreneurially. When we act in an entrepreneurial way, we empower ourselves to live the life we desire. These skills can then be applied to numerous disciplines, be it starting a business, following a dream career, pursuing a vocation, creating and producing a form of art – the choices are endless.

In my TEDx talk 'Why Teaching Entrepreneurial Skills in Schools is Essential' (https://youtu.be/HA-TFRXRWPY), I speak about the need to instil permission in our children to pursue what they want to do by developing their curiosity and encouraging creativity. Children don't need to grow up being held back by fear and limiting beliefs. Unleashing our entrepreneurial spirit gives us access to a way of living that empowers individuals, societies, communities, children and humanity. It is our duty.

HOW TO MAKE A GAME-CHANGING IMPACT

As I have already mentioned, entrepreneurship is not just about business; it's also a way of thinking. But not all entrepreneurs think and act in the same way. It is a myth that all entrepreneurs are 'Game Changers'. However, all entrepreneurs can make a game-changing impact.

You can now identify what kind of impact you can make as an entrepreneur by completing the Entrepreneur Impact Profile. The Entrepreneur Impact Profile shows how everyone can make a game-changing impact in their own way

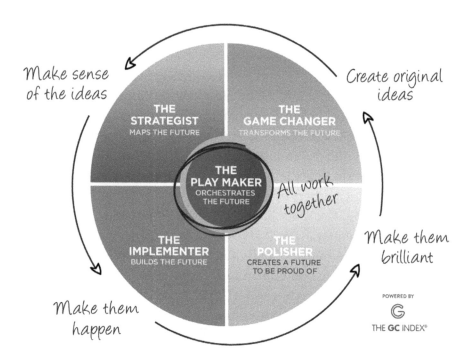

The Entrepreneur Impact Profile is powered by The GC Index®, a tool that has been used in the corporate market. The findings of the GC Index's research can be found in *The DNA of a Game Changer* (2015) and *The DNA of a Game-Changing Team* (2016).

We are living through the age of disruption. We can't flourish if we are content with things as they are, or even by making our offering a little better than everyone else's. Today, the most successful businesses don't just compete against their rivals to capture greater market share, they redefine the terms of competition by constantly transforming what they are doing and how they are doing it. Agility and acting quickly are critical to survival.

FOUR CRITICAL STEPS

Groundbreaking creativity and innovation may lie within an individual, but it takes a game-changing team to achieve long-term transformation. Think of Boeing, Google and Apple as examples of successful game-changing teams.

In today's digital world, we need to carry on with business as usual while we challenge ourselves to invent, implement and execute creative change. The key to success is to transform individual action into collective power. Not everyone is a game changer, but everyone can follow four steps to make a game-changing impact.

1. Develop strong values. It is worthwhile spending time developing a set of strong values to show what you stand for. Employees and customers will buy into your vision, share your values, and help you turn great ideas into reality.

Strong values position your proposition and help you build your team. When you communicate strong values, you will attract the kind of people who match your values and want to be part of your vision, which is the perfect way to identify the talent you need around you.

2. Focus on how you can make an impact. You can make an impact through:

- People – enabling everyone
- Ideas – exploring possibilities and making sense of them
- Tasks – getting things done efficiently and well

Now is the time to focus on the real impact that you can make personally as well as with others in your team. Focus on who is best for the job at hand. By understanding how each person will make an impact through their ideas and the actions they take, you can ensure they contribute to the team, project and wider organisation, making you far more likely to create a game-changing culture.

3. Identifying talent. Once you understand how you make your impact, it's important to identify the talent you need in your team. The right people in your team will help you make a game-changing impact as an entrepreneur.

The Entrepreneur Impact Profile (see www.EnSpirit. Global) provides entrepreneurs and business owners with a groundbreaking framework to identify the right talent. It empowers them to maximise their awareness of the contributions that they make and helps them understand their entrepreneurial strengths. This enables them to accelerate their impact on the world with some extraordinary results.

The Entrepreneur Impact Profile is powered by the GC Index®, which was created by Dr John Mervyn-Smith and Prof. Adrian Furnham following the launch of 'The DNA of a Game Changer' study.

The Entrepreneur Impact Profile (EIP):

- Measures how you make your best impact in the world as a business owner or entrepreneur

- Gives you a framework to ask the direct questions that maximise your impact

- Identifies how each team member will contribute to the team and organisation
- Helps you to create entrepreneurial game-changing teams and safe-to-fail cultures
- Creates a talent management framework that is inclusive and drives tangible business impact

The Entrepreneur Impact Profile is made up of five key roles:

1. **The Game Changer** – transforms the future (sees possibilities)

2. **The Strategist** – maps the future (sees patterns)

3. **The Implementer** – builds the future (sees practicalities)

4. **The Polisher** – creates a future to be proud of (sees potential)

5. **The Playmaker** – orchestrates the future (sees people)

As an entrepreneur or business owner, you cannot create anything great in the world without the right team working with you. It's often the dynamic of the team that moves things on and creates transformational change.

Understanding your profile is a liberating experience as you then know what you need to focus on and who you need around you. Do you need someone who can understand what needs to be done now – an implementer? Do you need someone to make things better – a polisher? Do you need someone to map out the future – a strategist?

4. Focus on culture. In today's fast-paced digital world, it's important for everyone within the business to feel they have the freedom to challenge things. We need everyone to be looking for new opportunities. We also need everyone to shift their mindsets to put impact at the heart of everything they do and make their own game-changing contribution.

These four critical steps will help to unleash the game-changing impact you can make on the world. The people who make a game-changing impact aren't superhuman. They don't have special powers; they are not born with an extra bit of something.

Since I have been running my own business, by observing my clients and being around some extraordinary people, I have found there are fundamental patterns to making a game-changing impact. The patterns fall into three categories which I call the three pillars.

THE THREE PILLARS

Pillar One is your inner game. It is all about what happens between your ears – your mindset; the context you live your life in; your thoughts; your feelings; how you deal with your emotions. All these have an impact on how you change the game.

Pillar Two is your game plan, your overall strategy. What does the big picture look like? Can you visualise what your life or business will look like in the future? I don't mean from a non-flexible point of view, but from a 'what I want my ideal life to look like' point of view.

Pillar Three is your outer game, the actions you take. Nothing happens without action, but what are the appropriate actions? What should you be doing, and when? How will you know if it is the right action?

Everything to do with your thoughts, feelings and emotions relates to you inner game – how you make decisions, the way you view the world, whom you trust, why you trust them, how you deal with failure, what you are afraid of, and how resilient you are. The worried mindset can make life really hard; the right mindset allows you to deal with things successfully. Many things happen in our lives that we have no control over, yet they have an impact on our thoughts, feelings and emotions. If we don't have the right mindset, we set ourselves up for misery, pain and heartache.

So what is the right mindset? In the book *Mindset: The New Psychology of Success*, Carol S. Dweck talks about the difference between a fixed mindset and a growth mindset. Someone with a fixed mindset has little room for growth, so to unleash your true entrepreneurial spirit and live a life you desire, you have to have a growth mindset. Imagine your quality of life if you embraced every challenge, kept on going when confronted with obstacles, looked to master new skills, took criticism on board and learnt from it, and were inspired by other people's success. The impact would be huge.

All the ideas in this book are conducive to developing a growth mindset. In fact, they require you to have a growth mindset. And the right mindset will lead you on to the right strategy.

Let me define strategy in the context of this book. It is more than just having plans around your goals; it's about looking at the bigger picture and understanding where the individual components fit in. How does each strategy work with the others to make the whole greater than the sum of the individual parts?

Highly successful people are not there by accident. There has to be some level of strategy involved, whether or not they are core to the team that works with them. A good game plan ensures long-term results.

It is easy to tell someone who doesn't have a strategy. They are just floating through life with a 'let's see what happens' attitude; nothing bad is happening, but nothing exciting is happening either. There is a fine line between being proactive, focusing on the now and taking appropriate action, and just seeing what happens and reacting accordingly. The difference is knowing your why.

Simon Sinek in his book and famous TEDx talk *Start With Why* illustrates that those who truly live their entrepreneurial spirit know why they do what they do. More importantly, they make sure others know why they do what they do, too. He gives numerous example of individuals and companies that have grown and prospered because people buy in to their why.

When you operate from your why, you unleash the true entrepreneurial spirit in you.

Alongside your growth mindset and game plan, it is essential that you take action. If you do nothing, nothing will happen. Every thought, feeling and emotion leads to some sort of action; the key is to ensure that the action you take serves you in achieving the life you desire. A fixed mindset will not select actions that serve you.

> 'Long-term consistency trumps short-term intensity.'
> — *Bruce Lee*

The size of the action you take is not important. If you take some action every day consistently, you will reap far more rewards than if you do nothing for periods of time then embark on a burst of action every now and then.

It's also not always about the action itself; it's more about the scope, confidence and access you get as a result of taking the action. For example, if you were to cut down on the amount of time you spend watching TV, how could this action help you change your game?

Mindset, strategy and action are all essential.

HOW TO USE THIS BOOK

The book is divided into three parts, each part covering one of the three pillars. You will find a total of fifty-six ideas for changing your game that don't require you to have money, a degree, or a privileged position. Anybody can implement them. I have been applying these ideas for over ten years to get consistent results, as have many other entrepreneurs.

You will need to focus on all three pillars; one without the other two will deliver indifferent results. For example, if you just concentrate on your inner game, nothing will ever happen as you will have no strategy and be taking no action. The best-laid plans can look great on paper, but they'll stay in the cupboard without the right mindset to take the right actions. And actions with no real direction will lead to inconsistencies and you won't learn from your mistakes.

If you use all three pillars, you will conquer your inner game and create a growth mindset. You won't be paralysed by analysis and you'll take action to keep moving forward. You'll have an overall game plan and know exactly where you are at any given point. Constantly developing your inner game, you will be able to adjust and pivot if the circumstances require you to do so.

This is when you truly start to change your game.

PILLAR ONE

THE INNER GAME

The True You

1. BE YOURSELF

This may seem obvious as surely we can't be any-thing but ourselves? However, sometimes the most obvious things are the ones we need to be reminded of in order to unleash our entrepreneurial spirit.

When we are born, we are like a blank sheet of paper. As we grow, we are given rules, conditions, patterns, parameters, limitations and behaviours to adhere to in order to conform to the society around us. The impact of this is that our dreams, wonder, curiosity, creativity and zest for life get numbed down. If we do try to be ourselves, we are often shot down – we are told to be quiet; get in line; it's not good to stand out. Growing up within this environment, we are faced with a continuous battle to be ourselves. It takes courage to step up every single day.

When you start to live through your entrepreneurial spirit, you give yourself permission to be yourself. When this occurs – and it will occur if you allow it to – it is the most liberating feeling in the world. Being you is just that. It is being authentic, being in your own power, being in the moment, and being accepted for the life you want to create. It requires no rulebooks, no conditions, no qualifications, no job interviews, and no social media followers.

When you open your eyes and see the world for what it really is, you will realise that there are many people out there being themselves. Think about the pop star who sings the kind of music which means a lot to them. They don't perform for their fans; they're performing for themselves, and their authenticity gets them the fans. Fans follow musicians, actors, sportspeople, etc, because those people's values resonate with them.

Here are some tips on how to go about being yourself:

Accept who you are. Embrace your desires, fears, strengths and weaknesses, moods and emotions. Ask five people to tell you what you are world class at. Trust what they say, absorb it, then ask yourself, 'If I were being that person, who would turn up each day?'

Write a letter to your childhood self. Find a photo of yourself when you were five years old and write a letter to that five-year-old, telling them who they can be and the kind of life they will create. Read this letter back to yourself on a weekly basis.

Imagine that you are on your deathbed. Think about the kind of things you would want people to say about you and list them. This list will reflect the true impact you want to have on the world. Now give yourself permission to be that person.

2. BEING AUTHENTIC

The definition of an authentic person is:

> 'Representing one's true nature or beliefs; true to oneself or to the person identified.'
> — www.dictionary.com

If you are not being authentic, then you are not being true to yourself.

It is easy to know when we are being authentic. It's a feeling; it's a way of being that flows within us. When we are trying to be or do something that doesn't feel right, we get an icky feeling. If we are *trying* to be authentic, by definition, we are not being authentic at all. That is the paradox.

The world we live in is a world of filters, statistics, content on social media, and people wanting to be something they are not. The opportunity here is that if you are truly authentic, you will be noticed among the abundance of fakeness. Make a game-changing impact by being as authentic as you can. So many people are trying to attract attention by being whatever they think the world wants to see, and in the process they are losing the very thing that people really want: the truth.

We cannot talk about authenticity without addressing situations and environment. How we turn up depends on the situation. This doesn't mean we are being inauthentic; we are simply being appropriate to the situation, be it at work, in a social setting, or at home with close family and friends. We can be authentic in different ways; there is no set formula. We will know when we are being authentic in a way that is appropriate to our environment, and we can see when someone else is not.

The good news is that it is much easier to be your true self than to be fake. Most people will accept the real you, and those who don't aren't the kind of people you want to be around anyway.

How can you be more authentic? By detecting when you are being inauthentic. That is the game changer. Being more aware of the feelings you have when you're in different situations and with different people will automatically lead to you being more authentic. Catch how you react to things; recognise feelings that repeat themselves. Being uncomfortable in a situation may be a sign that you're being inauthentic, but it's not always the case. There are times when the real you can be uncomfortable, maybe in a networking situation where you are talking to people you don't know.

Authenticity is all about being bold. Situations that challenge you will help you to grow, even if you do feel uncomfortable to begin with, but make sure you are being real in all these situations. Be as present as you can. When you are present, you prevent the past coming into the equation, bringing with it all the 'should' behaviours you have learnt over time. 'Should' behaviours do not demonstrate the real you and bring on inauthenticity.

The final aspect of being truly authentic is to accept your vulnerability. Nobody is perfect; we all have flaws, so trying to show the world a perfect persona is in itself inauthentic. The power is in showing the world that you are human and accepting who you are, come what may.

3. UNDERSTAND WHY YOU WERE BORN

If life isn't for living, what is it for? When we understand what we were born to do, everything becomes easy. Life flows, everything slots into place, opportunities appear, people seem nicer and life is grand.

Understanding why you were born is about understanding your life's true purpose. It's a shame that so many people settle for the mundane, for the safety of the ordinary in their lives.

Finding your true purpose isn't as hard as it may seem. It's always been within you, but society, the educational system and cultural expectations tend to envelope you, suppressing your purpose along with your dreams. Your duty is to rediscover your purpose.

You may already know your purpose, so now your challenge is to live it. Your purpose is linked to your values – what lights the fire in your belly? What comes easily to you? When you are in the zone and in flow, you are living your purpose.

One indicator of someone who is living their purpose without compromise is if they are achieving great things without money being their main motivator. Anyone living in the entrepreneurial spirit is living their purpose. That is not to say money is unimportant; we need it to live and grow. But when our sole purpose is to earn money, we can create an empty existence.

CASE STUDY – CHRIS BRANCH

Chris Branch is an osteopath by profession, but he is much more than that.

Chris contacted me to get some coaching to discover what his real purpose is. He wanted to know what drives him to do what he does. He felt that running his own osteopath clinic was too small a goal.

Through the coaching, we explored what playing the big game really looks like, and what that would mean to him. From an early age, he had known he wanted to help people, and through a series of life events, he'd ended up training as an osteopath. Although he knew he was doing what he'd set out to do, care for people, the vehicle for doing so didn't fulfil his why.

As it turned out, his why is to be the catalyst for a holistic way of living. Now Chris is not only a clinic owner, he is a blogger, speaker and health coach. Through exploring the essence of what he was doing, he has made a game-changing impact on the world.

When your purpose and your passion are aligned to generate profit, this is called your sweet spot. Take Hollywood actor Jim Carey as an example. His purpose is to make the world a pleasanter place through laughter, and the way he does that is through making blockbuster films.

'If you do what you love, you'll never work a day in
your life.'
— *Marc Anthony*

There's a great exercise you can download at www.
EnSpirit.Global/resources. Doing this exercise will
enable you to identify your core three values, which
will give you clarity on your purpose in life.

Looking at your core values, think about the kind
of professions that would allow you to fulfil them.
When you do work that directly links to your purpose, the rewards look after themselves. And they
don't always come to you in the way you may expect.
When you associate yourself with people who have
similar values and purposes to you, it makes it easier
to understand why you were born.

Your action now is to find three events or workshops
that you can attend which are aligned to your purpose. Once you've done this, I would like to invite
you to come to the private Facebook group and let
us know which events you will be attending: www.
facebook.com/EnSpiritGlobal

Time Is Precious

4. RESPECT TIME

Irrespective of who you are, there are always going to be people who are older than you and younger than you, richer than you and poorer than you, more knowledgeable than you and less knowledgeable than you. However, the one indisputable thing we all have is the same amount of time – twenty-four hours a day, seven days a week, fifty-two weeks per year. But some people are able to achieve so much more in the same amount of time than other people. Why is that?

The answer is respect. The achievers respect the time they have and know what they need to do within that time.

What would you do if you were given £86,400 each day? There are 86,400 seconds in a day, so how do you really make each second count?

OK, let's take into account that we sleep for eight hours and spend eight hours doing what we want to do, but that still leaves 28,800 seconds each day. You will never get that time back, but many people live their lives as if they can bank time like they bank their money and use it when they're ready. But there will come a time when it is too late and an opportunity has passed them by. As with so many things, they won't realise what they had until it is no longer with them.

Live every day like it is your last. This will allow you to respect time and be as productive as possible. No more regrets.

To see how respecting time can have a massive impact on how effective and productive you are, look at what the great entrepreneurs have achieved in the same amount of time as we have available to us.

The late Stephen Hawking, although not an entrepreneur in the traditional sense, was very much an entrepreneur in the way he thought about his life and his gift to the world. He did not allow his illness to hold him back in his pursuit of understanding how the universe works, and the massive contribution he made to the world of science is testament to his healthy respect for the time he had. He stayed true to his core purpose so others could benefit from his insights.

Richard Branson has over thirty companies running under the Virgin brand. His ability to build his companies and ensure that he has the right personnel in place is directly related to how he sees time and what he wants to do with it. It would be easy to look at entrepreneurs like Richard Branson and assume they are workaholics, working every hour of the day. Although they may work for more hours than most people, the real yardstick of their success is how impactful they are with their time.

When you are using your time effectively, try not to look at it as time management. Time is constantly moving forward, and whatever you are doing is moving forward with it. It is impossible to manage something that is moving outside of your control.

What you are managing is yourself. Therefore, time management is actually all about self-management – how disciplined you are, how effective you are, and how productive you are with the time you make available for yourself.

5. CONTROL YOUR NEWS CONSUMPTION

If you are as old as I am, you may remember a time when there were only four TV channels, and the news was on four times during the day: at breakfast time, lunchtime, early evening, and ten o'clock at night. These were the only televised opportunities people had to find out what was going on in the world.

Now we have twenty-four hour news channels, internet feeds, social media channels, as well as the traditional press and radio stations. We don't have to go looking for the news; the news finds us. But how does hearing the news serve us? Does it actually serve us at all? Probably not.

I am not presenting some conspiracy theory here about the news agencies being controlled by a central government body to make us think and believe in a certain way; this is about us not buying into the fear generated by 'bad news'. The constant dialogue of what is wrong with the world sensationalises stories to be more than they really are.

The other dynamic at work here is that it's no longer just the media agencies that communicate the news; everyone can be news reporters. With social media, we have the power to communicate what is happening, often much more quickly than professional journalists. As soon as something happens, we can be sure there will be pictures and video put up on social media platforms within seconds. People on the other side of the world can hear about it as quickly as someone in the next city.

We can also choose which type of news we want to come to us. What to know the football scores? Set up a feed. Want to know stock prices? Set up a notification. Want to know breaking news? Set up a Google alert.

My challenge to you now is not to watch any news or read any newspapers for a week and see how your mind starts to function. Of course, the impact of this challenge will depend on how much you watch and read the news at the moment. The mind is like a sponge: it will absorb whatever information you expose it to. Don't tell it stories about what is going wrong in the world; give it information that allows it to grow and make game-changing contributions.

6. BALANCE – MOVE, BREATHE AND MEDITATE

Balance in your life is essential. You can't work all the time; you can't play all the time; you can't study for eight hours without taking a break. However, the modern world sometimes seems like it expects you to be driving towards a goal at one hundred miles an hour; otherwise, you will not be seen as being committed. But this will only lead to one thing: burnout.

I used to meditate now and again, mainly as a tick-box exercise to say I had done it. But that was before I went on a yoga and meditation retreat in India. What I learnt on this trip was that balance is the key to all success. We need our health, we need to have clarity, and we need to be free of anxiety to be at our best. And the way to achieve this is to have a balance between body and mind through physical exercise, controlled breathing and meditation.

My physical exercise comes from yoga poses, or asana. Intentional breathing, or pranayama, is all about control. Meditation, if done properly, allows my mind to clear and frees it of thoughts, allowing me to be more relaxed and have peace of mind and greater clarity.

When you move your body, as well as the obvious health benefits, it also has an impact on your mind. Yoga's discipline requires you to concentrate the mind while you are doing the physical exercises. This aligns the movement with what your mind is concentrating on. For example, with each move, you may concentrate on either your inhaling or your exhaling, depending on the pose.

Yoga practice means that you give your full attention to one specific activity, which is something people rarely do in the modern world. This complete attention will help you to be more productive. The physical activity you choose doesn't have to be yoga, but I have found the combination of yoga poses, breathing and mediation to be the best method of practising complete attention.

Controlling your breathing, which is what I like to call 'intentional breathing', can help with clearing your mind, getting you centred with internal balance. In yoga terms, it is called pranayama. If you look at how a baby breathes, you will see their whole stomach expand from the diaphragm. The key to pranayama is to breathe like a baby. Take a few minutes a day to focus on your breathing and allow your mind to clear. I find it best to do this before I meditate properly.

Breathing exercises can help you relax, as they make your body feel like it does when you are already relaxed. I would advise you to read *The Mind–Body Mood Solution* by Jeffrey Rossman for detailed steps on how to engage in slow diaphragmatic breathing. Deep breathing is one of the best ways to lower stress in the body. When you breathe deeply, it sends a message to your brain to calm down.

Meditation has also been scientifically proven to help relieve stress, improve concentration and increase wellbeing. For the eastern world, meditation is as natural and important as breathing, and the western world is starting to adopt the practice, but many are still sceptical about it. All I would advise you to do is try meditation, and if you see the benefits in your everyday life, carry on. If you meditate as a tick-box exercise but don't see any benefits during the day, then it may not be for you. Try meditation for three weeks then make a judgement call.

What can meditation help you with? It boosts your health by:

- Strengthening your immune system
- Increasing your positive emotion
- Enhancing your emotional intelligence
- Increasing social awareness
- Helping you control your emotions
- Improving your productivity
- Increasing your focus and attention
- Improving your memory
- Developing your creativity
- Decreasing depression
- Decreasing anxiety
- Reducing stress
- Improving your perspective
- Making you feel happy
- Increasing your energy

When you meditate, you observe your mind and realise you don't have to be a slave to it. Meditation allows you to clear out the junk, tune in to your talents, and connect with yourself. One of the most common and simplest ways to do this is to listen to music. Let the tune absorb you and your thoughts.

For me, meditation is a reset for the day and a decluttering of the mind so I can be at my most productive. We can't control what happens around us, but we do have a say over the quality of our mind. When we have inner balance, we will be able to deal with anything we encounter from the outside world. No matter what's going on, if our mind is OK, everything is OK.

We will talk more about meditation in Pillar Three.

Go With The Flow

7. LEARN TO ACCEPT FAILURE

If you are reading this, you are someone who has failed at some things in your life. You will fail again, and then you will fail some more. Those who accept that failure is a part of the journey have already succeeded.

> 'If you're not prepared to be wrong, you'll never come up with anything original.'
> — *Ken Robinson*

> 'Failure should be our teacher, not our undertaker... Failure is something we can avoid only by saying nothing, doing nothing, and being nothing.'
> — *Denis Waitley*

'It's failure that gives you the proper perspective on success.'
    — *Ellen DeGeneres*

'Success is not final, failure is not fatal: it is the courage to continue that counts.'
    — *Winston Churchill*

'There is only one thing that makes a dream impossible to achieve: the fear of failure.'
    — *Paulo Coelho*

'It's not how far you fall, but how high you bounce that counts.'
    — *Zig Ziglar*

This last quote says it all. Success is never about avoiding failure; it's always about bouncing back.

CASE STUDY – GERT SCHOLTS

A lot of my early work was in training sales psychology to sales teams and creating an edge in the market, ensuring they could be the best of the best. Gert Scholts contacted me to explore ways to get the best from his teams. They were already top performers, but he knew some of the team members could be performing even better.

After working with the teams for a few weeks, I realised that some of the team members were afraid to fail. This avoidance of failure at all costs meant they didn't ask crucial questions, they were often speaking to

non-decision makers, and lead time was longer than it
needed to be. A simple shift in mindset allowed them to
go after the deals without holding anything back. Yes,
they lost some sales, but the learning they got from
their mistakes taught them far more valuable lessons
than they would have gained by playing safely.

If you don't accept failure, you will never reach your
true potential and be able to unleash your entrepreneurial spirit.

No one likes disappointment, but actually, it's fine.
You can look back at where you failed, feel glad you
went through it, and learn. In every failure, there is a
lesson. Accepting and learning from that lesson will
set you up for success.

There is a body of research that suggests frequent
and fast failure is the best route to success. Decision
science and data analytics firm, Mu Sigma, demonstrates scientifically that failure drives innovation
forward.

> 'The rapid change of pace in business puts companies
> under pressure to innovate constantly. New
> technologies are making it possible to meet this
> challenge through ongoing experimentation.'
>   — Tom Pohlmann, head of strategy and
>   value at Mu Sigma

Pohlmann says that failing isn't bad for business. Instead, it leads to something else happening, which, if carried out correctly builds upon that failure.

> 'It forces companies to shed predetermined concepts and switch to a mode of constant experimentation and learning.'
> — *Tom Pohlmann, head of strategy and value at Mu Sigma*

With the speed at which technology is moving, companies and entrepreneurs cannot succeed without failing. In some industries, by the time you think of an idea, innovate it and take it to market, it may already be a failure because new technologies have been developed. You have to innovate on the go and fail to succeed. For Pohlmann, innovation is often like throwing darts at a moving dartboard: you can either try to throw the darts more accurately, or throw more of them to increase the probability of hitting the bull's eye.

There are three things you have to be aware of when dealing with failure:

- Failure is not fatal; you have another chance

- You will become a better person for it, even if it doesn't feel like it at the time

- Any great innovation is littered with failed attempts, so welcome the opportunity to fail

8. BE DIFFERENT

Our DNA shows we are unique in every respect. There is nobody in the world like us – even identical twins are individuals.

As we grow, we develop our own perspective on the world. The argument over whether it is genetics or the environment that plays more of a part in forming us as an individual has gone on for centuries, and it will continue. Even when siblings are brought up in the same way in the same environment, they can still turn out differently.

When we enter society, first through the schooling system and then through our careers, we get bombarded by messages telling us that we have to fit in, conform to a norm, not stand out, follow the crowd, play it safe, not take any silly risks. Essentially, we are told not to be different. We are conditioned through school, the news and general society that if we stray from the norm, if we stand out too much, if we go against the crowd, we will be ridiculed. We will be seen as a disruptive influence. As a result, we find it difficult to accept anyone or anything that looks different or is seen as different.

You cannot change your game if you stay the same as everyone else.

My question to you is: how does it make you feel when you stand out and deviate from the norm? Alive? Noticed? Valued? Respected as an individual? Seen as someone who has a unique gift?

No, I didn't think so.

The system is not designed to celebrate our differences. When people do break the mould and try something different, initially they are mocked. They are told they can't do whatever they want to do. But if they persist and achieve something different, then all of a sudden everyone admires them for having the courage to be innovative.

The inner drive that makes you come alive is your difference. The core of unleashing your entrepreneurial spirit is to be different. You can't be anything else. If you conform, you die while still being alive.

I want you to give yourself permission to be different. By reading this book, you are in fact starting to be different. Can you think of anyone, famous or not, who has blended in and been the same as everyone else and achieved what they wanted to achieve? It's just not possible to unleash your inner spirit unless you celebrate your differences.

What happens when you accept that you are different and were born to stand out? For a start, you will stop comparing yourself to others. How can you possibly compare yourself to anyone when there is only one of you? You have a gift – the thing that allows you to feel alive; the thing you were put on this earth to be – and when you accept your difference, the world will benefit.

History is littered with examples of people who chose to be different and stand out: Martin Luther King, Mahatma Gandhi, Bill Gates, Usain Bolt, Oprah Winfrey, Mary Kay, Pelé, Anita Roddick, Princess Diana, Stephen Covey, Henry Ford, Jessica Ennis, JK Rowling, Dele Alli – the list goes on. For them, it was the only way to be. But imagine what the world would be like if these people hadn't chosen to be different. What will your life be like if you are too afraid to be different?

To be different, you have to step out and expand your comfort zone. It will seem hard at first, but once you realise the benefits, both to you and the world, there will be no stopping you.

Let's investigate how you can achieve this.

Choose. Choose to be different. Choose to acknowledge that there is no one else like you. Choose never to feel like you have to conform and be the same as everyone else again.

Make a commitment to a project. You can only truly self-express when you commit to something bigger than yourself. This commitment could be a career move, starting a new venture, or starting a project, for example. The key thing here is that when you commit to something bigger than yourself, it is no longer about you.

Stop comparing yourself with others. You have no idea what other people are truly like or what challenges they have in their lives. You only see what they choose to show you.

We are all in different chapters of our lives, so when you compare yourself to other people, you may be comparing your Chapter 1 with their Chapter 6. Or you may be on Chapter 8 and you are comparing yourself to someone else's Chapter 3, even if they may seem on the surface to be ahead of you in life.

> 'The person who follows the crowd will usually go no further than the crowd. The person who walks alone is likely to find himself in places no one has ever seen before.'
> — *Albert Einstein*

Stay in your own lane, do your own thing, and show the world what you are made of. Stop following the crowd; the crowd is only following someone else. You will never feel alive this way.

There is some good news: most people will stay the same. They will be consumed by society's rules and what they falsely believe to be what life is about. This leaves massive opportunities open for those who do take action, do believe in themselves, and do want to take the chance to be who they were born to be. Being different is not about being rebellious; it is about being true to who you are and living a life you desire. By taking this chance, you can really stand out.

If you haven't already done so, come and join the Game Changer's Facebook group: www.facebook. com/EnSpiritGlobal. Complete the statement 'I am different because…' and add it to a post with a picture of you holding this book.

9. HAVE FAITH IN YOUR ABILITIES

Faith is what is left when belief has gone. There are many people who don't have complete belief in themselves, but they keep the faith.

Belief will come and go. Keeping your faith will ensure you don't make rash, emotionally led decisions. There will be circumstances where you will find it hard to believe in yourself and what you can achieve. By keeping the faith, you will allow yourself to deal with setbacks well.

It is often the case that people around you will believe in your abilities more than you believe in yourself. This helps to keep your faith high.

We have the ability to achieve anything we want, but we need the environment, the strategy and the faith to make it count. Many people never realise their true potential because they are not in the right environment. They don't have the right people around them, they lack the confidence to ask for help, or they just don't have faith in what they can achieve. That is one of the main reasons why I am writing this book – it will give you a resource to keep your faith high. You can dip in and out, read any tip again, and it will hopefully give you the boost you need.

Keeping faith with your abilities means you trust the process of how things work out. Success leaves clues and patterns, and any obstacles you encounter in your life are not new. They will all have been encountered by someone else before you, so it follows that solutions to every obstacle and problem already exist, too. There is nothing that you will face in life that cannot be dealt with.

10. BE IN YOUR FLOW

'Do not dwell in the past, do not dream of the future, concentrate the mind on the present moment.'
— *Buddha*

Flow is when you are totally immersed in a task and completely forget about the outside world. When you are in your flow, work is effortless. Time flies and you don't feel like you are even working; you are just being. You are truly in your excellence; you are in your perfect space where you produce your best work; you don't have to think what to do or how to be. This is the space that you could happily stay in for ever.

The concept of flow was first developed by Dr Mihaly Csikszentmihalyi. In fact, Dr Csikszentmihalyi went as far as saying that being in flow contributes to a life worth living.

His study of flow started from examining the roots of happiness by looking at World War II veterans dealing with life after the war. He wanted to understand where in their everyday lives they experienced true happiness. What he discovered was that the feeling they experienced when they were performing certain tasks was akin to ecstasy. They felt like they were observing themselves performing the task; they felt like the outside world no longer existed.

It was this state that Dr Csikszentmihalyi called 'flow'.

Working on this book, I knew I had to get in my flow in order to get it written and published. The good news is that there are certain conditions we can create to get into flow. For me specifically, I would wake up at 5am, get showered, drink a pint of water, then sit from 5.30am until 7am. I put some of my favourite music on and made sure the room felt cosy. I would research the topic I was going to be writing about for twenty to thirty minutes, and then I'd start writing. No editing, no pauses, just writing.

The discipline of waking up early and creating certain conditions made it easy for me to get in flow. Knowing what would occur, I had no trouble waking up at 5am each day, because I knew that as a result of getting into my flow, I would write another 1,000 words.

Dr Mihaly Csikszentmihalyi found that there are seven feelings that occur when you are in flow:

- Your concentration is focused; you feel completely involved in the task

- You have clarity. You just know what needs to be done and you do it

- You know the task to be doable. You feel the skills you have are more than capable of completing the task

- You feel ecstatic – it's like you are outside your reality

- It's intrinsic. The activity itself produces flow, becoming the reward

- You feel serene. You have no anxieties; you feel at one with yourself

- Time flies; hours feel like minutes

If this is what flow looks and feels like, why wouldn't everybody want to be in flow as much as possible?

Seven ways you can get into flow:

1. Be clear what you want to achieve. If you have clarity over exactly what you want, flow will be easier to achieve. Writing this book, I have a clear deadline, I have a clear word target, and most importantly, I have a clear reason for writing it, so getting into flow is easy.

2. Eliminate distractions. To get a clear head and maximise flow, you need to clear the space around you of all distractions. Turn off notifications, clear your desk, and make sure the room is quiet and comfortably warm. Music that helps your focus is a useful tool, and there are now apps that play music over a focused period of time to help you get into flow.

3. Make sure your task is important. The task you choose has to be meaningful. When you complete it, you need to know you have achieved something of worth; something big that will make an impact.

4. Make it challenging. The task needs to challenge you enough to stretch you and require your full concentration, but not so much that you can't do it. It will be the kind of task that helps you gain more and more confidence in your ability the more you do it.

5. Choose something you love. You have got to want to do it. If you dread the task and will do anything to avoid it, you won't ever be in flow when you do it.

6. Find your focused time. Are you a morning person or a night owl? I am definitely not a morning person, but I found that when I created the right conditions, I could get into flow in the morning. But it had to be for a focused period of time. Those ninety minutes before I started writing allowed me to get 1,000 words down each day, and knowing I had achieved that made my day much better. Whatever happened, I had already achieved something meaningful before my day even started properly.

7. Be aware of your emotions. Self-awareness is a great indicator of flow. How do you feel? If you are having trouble getting into flow, make a check of your emotions. Are you feeling anxious? Angry? Worried about something? If this is the case, don't try to force flow – it can't be forced, but you can create feelings and circumstances that make it easier to get there. Walk away, drink some water, relax, then go again.

There is no perfect time to get into flow. Sometimes it just happens, but to make it happen, you need the discipline to create the right circumstances.

11. ACCEPT YOUR GIFT

We are all born with something unique, our gift. The thing that makes us different. Don't kid yourself, you have a gift, and it's likely that others can see it in you, even if you can't. The drive you have inside you, the spirit that makes you feel alive, is the core of your gift. It is your genius, how you flow when you are in the zone.

Can you remember a time in your life when you felt completely connected with what you were doing? This is your gift. How you manifest this gift and bring it to the world is part of showing up and changing your game. But before I show you how you can identify your gift, you have to accept that you have one.

This acceptance can be a big thing in itself. You may be someone who naturally doesn't like to show off, but accepting your gift is not about showing off. It's about understanding that the gift you have is a present for someone else.

Imagine for one moment that all the people you admire, either from a professional or personal perspective, hadn't accepted their gifts and shown up in the world. Imagine if Pelé had not accepted his gift with a football, Mozart his gift for composing, Richard Branson his gift for seeing opportunities,

Martin Luther King his gift to be the leader of a movement, and Michael Jackson his gift for singing and performing. What a travesty this would have been.

It's important here to point out that you don't have to become famous or change the world. Your gift could be to listen, to make a difference to a select few people, to educate, to create products, to make things, to play a musical instrument, to heal the sick, to write, to cook, or to be the catalyst for change. It doesn't matter how big or small your gift is, as long as it moves you and draws out your passion.

It is your duty to discover what your gifts are and show them to the world. This is part of changing your game. You may need to go on a journey of self-discovery to find your gift. For me, personal development allowed me to discover, accept and bring my gifts to the world. And I'm still discovering them, which is the really exciting part.

12. BE GRATEFUL

Being grateful is appreciating what we have. When we are not grateful, we concentrate on what we lack or what we have lost. We also look at what others have.

There are 7.5 billion people on the planet. In our lifetime, according to Funders and Founders, we will meet around 80,000 of them. That is 0.0001% of the world's population. When we appreciate that we will only ever meet 0.0001% of the world's population in our lifetime, we realise we have no idea what other people's lives are like, so we need to be grateful for what we have. It is all we can really do.

Being grateful is such a powerful attitude to have. You want to change your game – I guess that is why you are reading this book! But I bet you have been guilty of at least one of the following:

- Comparing yourself with others – thinking others have achieved more than you

- Thinking that you're not good enough – believing you need more knowledge

- Worrying a lot – worrying never changes a situation; if anything, it makes you think things are worse than they really are

- Having high expectations – high standards are good, but being attached to high expectations leads to upset

- Being busy – always on the go; never stopping; no time to enjoy life

- Feeling entitlement – you have what you deserve; feeling entitled kills your happiness

- Believing you must be perfect – striving for perfection means you never see the beauty in anything; nothing will ever be perfect, so get used to it

If you really want to change the game, be grateful for all that you have. When you are grateful, your world changes. You start to live from an empowered position rather than a position of lacking. From this empowered position, you are free to create because your focus is not on what you don't have.

Practising gratitude is something many people don't appreciate until they try it. Research by Robert Emmons, editor of the *Journal of Positive Psychology*, found that when you express gratitude, your mental, physical and relational wellbeing improve enormously. Being grateful directly impacts happiness.

Does striving for success bring more happiness, or does being happy bring more success? From my experience, I believe being happy brings more success, which is why gratitude is so important.

Here are eight benefits of gratitude:

1. You will have an optimistic outlook on life.
2. Your emotional, social and physical wellbeing will improve.
3. You will forgive more easily.
4. It will decrease your levels of stress and illness.
5. You will care about yourself more.

6. You emotional and intellectual intelligence will improve.

7. You will deal with loss better.

8. You will know life is not all about you; it is bigger than you.

It is amazing when we look at the many benefits of gratitude that this is not widely practised. When we appreciate what we have, we feel better, but a lot of this appreciation is at a surface level. Practising gratitude at a deep level is a game changer.

Am I saying you need to spend all day being thankful? Not really. The key is to use gratitude as the foundation for your day. Journaling, which we will talk about in more detail later in the book, is a great way of recording your gratitude for what is in your life.

With gratitude, you start to feel the internal benefits within days. You will feel less stressed and anxious as you will stop worrying about things outside your control; you will feel lighter. Gratitude is attractive. Over a period of time, other people will see a different aura about you. They will want to be around you as it feels good to be with you. Gratitude will be the invisible force that brings the right people, opportunities and energy in to your life.

Here are five ways you can practise gratitude:

1. Commit to it every day. With consistence and persistence, you will see the benefits of gratitude after a period of time.

2. Journal each day – see the chapter entitled 'Stay Ahead' for more detail.

3. See the good in everything – all people, all circumstances and all things. There is a silver lining in everything you do. People whose cup is always half full can practise this step without thought.

4. Smile more. When you smile, others see your gratitude. It is also a great way to connect with them.

5. When you see the positive results of gratitude, don't stop. It needs to be an ongoing practice.

Embrace Change

13. UNLEARN EVERYTHING

Unlearn everything? Isn't this counterintuitive? On the surface, it can seem so.

From birth, we learn how to react to sounds, faces, feelings. When we start to move, we learn how to crawl, then walk. When we start to speak, we learn how to communicate with sounds, then words. When we go to school, we learn facts and figures. When we start work, we learn how to master our job and earn a living. But at what stage do we learn how to be our authentic selves?

Our brain is programmed in a way that allows us to function in the world. But as we progress through life, it is also programmed to suppress our instincts, our dreams, our risk-taking, our adventurous nature. We learn to think and act in a way that will allow us to survive, not thrive.

Think about the brain as a computer and each life lesson as a software installation. In our formative years, our personalities are developing. The way we react, think, act and create for the rest of our life is largely determined in the first eleven years of our life. This is when we decide:

- What we believe is possible for us

- How we react to fear

- How risk averse we will be

- Whether we will be the type of person who will do the things we believe to be possible

- How other people will see us

- What our role will be in society

The way we are is not free will; we are operating from the anchor of the learnings, the 'software' we installed in our brain at the start of our life. Our first eleven years teach us how to operate for conventional living. The rules are strict, hard and constrained – not at all conducive to unleashing our entrepreneurial spirit and changing our game. In order to unleash the spirit inside us, the spirit that drives us, our true essence, we have to reprogram our internal software.

> 'Empty your cup so that it may be filled; become devoid to gain totality.'
> — *Bruce Lee*

Bruce Lee was not only a master of martial arts, but also a master of the mind. You mind is currently filled with how you believe you should act, think, feel, fear, achieve, and there is no room to expand. With old software, you can only go so far, so you now have to learn how to unlearn. You have to uninstall the out-of-date software and install new software.

Take a smartphone, for example. Every few weeks, it will ask you to install a software upgrade. Why? Because in a bunker somewhere, a group of techies is collecting data on how your phone's current software is operating and finding new ways to make it work more efficiently. Once you upgrade, your phone will operate more quickly and smoothly, and you will be able to use it to do things that it previously couldn't do.

How do you unlearn everything to upgrade to being your true self? The tips in this book will help, but there are three key things you can do.

1. Surround yourself with inspirational people. Who do you aspire to be? Who lives up to your standards?

> 'You are the average of the five people you spend the most time with.'
> — *Jim Rohn, author, entrepreneur and motivational speaker*

Start spending time with people who lift your average.

2. Watch TED videos. www.TED.com is a fantastic resource with great insights and thought-provoking talks on every subject you can imagine. These are not talks by professional speakers, but by people who look at the world in a different way and have a take on a subject that most of us would never have thought of.

Listening to one TED talk a day will help you unlearn what you think you know about the world and understand what you are capable of.

3. Have a purpose.

> 'The two most important days in your life are the day you are born and the day you find out why.'
> — *Mark Twain*

I am assuming you know the day on which you were born, but do you know why you were born? What is your true purpose? Are you pursuing it?

Having and pursuing a purpose is one of the most liberating things you can do. It can only happen once you unlearn what you believe to be true.

My purpose is to create a society that thinks in an entrepreneurial way in order for people to create and pursue a life they desire. I fulfil my purpose through the books I write, the EnSpirit.Global platform, the Global Impact Network, the courses, the training I provide, and the partnerships I have around the world. For me to create all this, I had to unlearn what I believed was possible for me and install new ways of thinking that allowed me to pursue my purpose.

The process of unlearning is the process of letting go. Let go of what you think is the right way of doing things, let go of what seems to be the norm, and let go of what you think will work. This seemingly counter-intuitive process will save you so much time.

Facts, processes, and systems are easy to replicate. With the internet, we have a vast amount of resources, but no amount of knowledge will be as powerful as going back to the core reason you were born, unleashing your entrepreneurial spirit, and living life on your own terms.

14. TRAIN YOUR THOUGHTS

Why is this important?

According to some schools of thought, you are what you think. Do you believe this? Well, it is true.

Emotions play a huge part in who you are. You cannot separate emotions and thoughts. Certain thoughts lead to certain emotions, and certain emotions lead to certain thoughts. You could say that training your thoughts is training your mind and training your emotions is training your heart.

Three great quotes explain this perfectly.

'Change your thoughts and you change your world.'
  — Norman Vincent Peale

You may say, 'What will change my world is more money / a better relationship / a better career. Changing my thoughts won't change anything', but here is the thing. *Nothing* in your life will change until you change your thoughts. The final step you want to take starts with the first step, and your first step is to change your thoughts about the situation.

When you change your thoughts, your perspective changes. You see things differently; it's like your filter changes. The situation you want to change is still the same, but *you* are now different. Your focus is going in a different direction, and only now can your situation change. It may take time because the devil on your shoulder will want to keep you seeing things as you first saw them, but with practice, you can change your thoughts. You *will* change them.

'To enjoy good health, to bring true happiness to one's family, to bring peace to all, one must first discipline and control one's own mind. If a man can control his mind he can find the way to Enlightenment, and all wisdom and virtue will naturally come to him.'
— *Buddha*

When you control your mind, you control your thoughts. But what does controlling your mind look like? It looks like this:

- You don't give in to temptation

- You don't procrastinate

- You respond, you don't react

- You see balance in the world

- You don't attach yourself to outcomes

- You never apportion blame

- You take total responsibility

The key here is that you take a stand, irrespective of what is happening around you.

'A man is but the product of his thoughts. What he thinks, he becomes.'
— *Mahatma Gandhi*

Most people want to:

- Be happy

- Be successful

- Be at peace

- Be wealthy

- Be content

- Be noticed

- Be valued

The focus on what we want to 'be' all too often starts with what we want, followed by what we have to do to get it. We list the things we want, for example a car, a house, love, money – lots of material stuff, and then we list the things we need to do to get those things. We believe that if we get what we want, we will be all of the things listed above.

You can actually be anything you want. When Mahatma Gandhi said we become what we think, he meant us to start with changing our inner thoughts, not the material things around us. Don't allow your thinking to be dictated by your environment, your past, your story, or your experiences. Create thoughts that empower you, make you authentic, and allow you to be the best version of yourself. The great thing about training your thoughts is that they are yours and yours alone.

When you focus on training your thoughts, you become able to respond rather than react. This is a game changer of huge significance. When you react to the world, your emotions take over and you operate from a foggy mindset. When you have awareness of your thoughts, you are able to respond wisely. Your actions are more considered. You pause before the response. You have calmness within. Changing your game starts when you respond to the world rather than making reactive, emotional decisions.

The good thing about training your thoughts is that it can be quite simple. But the bad thing about training your thoughts is also that it can be quite simple. Often we assume that something which is simple won't get big results. But most of the troubles in the world have come about as a result of ill-thought-out reactions that led to bad communications, bad decisions, and assumptions.

Here are five ways to train your thoughts.

1. Create a gratitude list. We talked about gratitude in the previous chapter. Creating a gratitude list focuses your mind on what you already have and not on what you don't have.

2. Focus on others. When you help other people, your focus is on them and you have to think about them. That's the space you need to be in.

3. Do what you love. When you focus on doing what you love, your thoughts follow. Following your passion means you reduce stress, you don't worry as much, and you are more likely to be in flow.

4. Meditate. Meditation calms your mind, centres you, and gives you perspective. When your mind is calm, often your brainwaves change, and then you can train your mind to respond to things in a calm and considered way.

5. Exercise and move. When you change your physical state and move, the mind has no time to wander. When you exercise, you release endorphins. These trigger a positive feeling in the body, similar to the effects of morphine.

In order to train your thoughts, you don't need to take a course, you don't need more money, you don't need anyone else's permission, and you can start now. The world will be at your feet the moment you change your thoughts.

15. CHANGE YOUR LANGUAGE

Words change the world. The words you use can make an impact on how people see you and how you see yourself. Language can influence behaviour and emotion. That's why the language you use is so important.

'Do, or do not. There is no try.'
   — *Yoda*, The Empire Strikes Back

Think about this quote. The language leaves no room for excuses. When Yoda said this in the film, he was telling Luke to commit either fully or not at all. There is no middle ground.

'Try' gives you an out. By allowing 'try' to be part of your language, you are essentially saying, 'I will try my best, but you cannot blame me if I don't succeed.' When you say 'do' there is no get-out clause. Those with an entrepreneurial mindset and approach to life don't set a scene where failure could be part of the outcome.

There are numerous studies that give you the science behind your language, thoughts and emotions, but the important point to understand is that certain words help you to have a positive mindset and thought process. Look to replace 'try' with 'will' or 'do'.

Another word that puts expectations on us is the word 'should'. 'Should' can leave us feeling like we are not enough, which is demotivating. When we use the word 'should' in our internal language, by implication we are saying we are not doing something important. When we use the word 'should' in our external language, we are forcing our view of the world on to someone else.

Imagine the impact in your world if you replaced 'should' with 'could', both in your internal and external vocabulary. For example, replace 'I should eat more healthily, but I don't know what to eat' with 'I could eat more healthily as I know it will make me feel better'; 'I should start that project for work, but I'm scared I'll get it wrong' with 'I could start that project and see what I can learn'; 'I should think about finding more time to do the things I want to do, but I am so busy with work and family' with 'What could I do to be more productive and present when I am working or with the family so that I can have more time to do the things I want?'

Look at your language – is it serving you? Does it give you the opportunity to move forward, or does it keep you stuck where you are?

16. BE COMFORTABLE BEING UNCOMFORTABLE

So many people resist change, whether it's because of fear of the unknown, not wanting to let go of what feels good now, or thinking the process of change will be too daunting. But in order to grow, be your true self and change your game, you have to accept change. In fact, you have to embrace change.

Life is constantly changing, but whether or not we grow from the changes is up to us. Recently, I was coaching a client who wanted a career change, but for the last seven years he had been overlooked for promotion. He had never even got a second interview.

After a frank conversation about what he wanted, what he was resisting, and what he was prepared to do, I realised that he had been living the same year, repeated seven times. Yes, he was now seven years older and seven years more experienced than when he'd first applied for promotion, but he hadn't done anything different year on year. He hadn't accepted any changes – there was always an excuse or a reason for him to resist, and he hadn't been prepared to look within himself to see why he wasn't getting the opportunities. This had cost him dearly.

Many of us want different things in life, to progress. We may even want to change, but at the same time we resist change. But accepting change is liberating. The fear of change is often unwarranted, as the results are never as bad as we may expect them to be.

There are two main reasons why you need to accept change.

1. It's inevitable. It's not optional, it's a guarantee. In life, things change, and you change. Sometimes, change is forced upon you, sometimes it's a conscious decision, but either way, change happens. Resisting it is futile. When you resist change, all you will do is increase your anxiety and stress.

2. Growth needs change. The very nature of growth means that things change. Resisting change will halt growth. At a surface level, this leads to frustration; at a deeper level, it can lead to depression and high levels of anxiety. Accepting change leads to growth, pleasure and a release of your inner spirit.

When change occurs, acknowledge it, accept it, and learn from it. What you learn from the experience will increase your wisdom, with the natural consequence that you will grow stronger. Reduce your expectations of what life should be and accept what could be.

Stop making change the enemy. Instead, make change your best friend.

Smell Opportunities

17. OWN YOUR SPACE

When you own your space, you are saying to the world, 'This is who I am, these are my values, and I am comfortable with that.' You are telling the world you are someone who matters and it needs to stand up and take notice. You will have an air of confidence that is almost tangible, a magnetic aura. When you walk into a room, people will want to be around you. They will feel good around you. You will have the X factor. It is nothing anyone can put their finger on, but they will know it when they see it.

When you own your space from a place of authenticity, there is no ego involved. It is not arrogance; you just believe in you. And people can tell the difference, which is why they will be attracted towards you.

When you do not own your space, you feel small and you look small. You go unnoticed because it looks to other people like you don't believe in yourself. Worse still, you may be looking for approval from others. When you own your space, you don't need anyone else's approval or permission. No justification is needed as you are just being you.

Owning your space makes it easy to change the game. Your focus when you own your space is 100% on making a game-changing impact, not worrying about whether you are doing the right thing, looking for approval, or being scared of failure.

CASE STUDY – SU PATEL

Su Patel is an HR professional who has worked within many organisations. Leaving school and going straight into the workplace, she worked her way up through the ranks and become respected within the corporate world.

A few years back, she started her own HR training and consultancy business to have more flexibility and to do what she wanted to do within HR. This was partly driven by life circumstances when she had children.

When I started working with Su, it soon became evident that she had a vast amount of knowledge and a unique, personable approach to HR. She was very much people rather than company centred, and her core drive was to help people, not just to make money. The issue Su had was how to show up in the world. How could she put herself out there as the go-to expert for other HR managers and professionals?

We worked on owning her space. How did we do this? By making it all about the people she wanted to serve. When she put herself into the equation and focused on owning her own space, she started to get the kind of feedback she craved.

People like to deal with people who know their stuff, but are coming from a place of humility. This is exactly how Su operates. She had been cautious of being seen as a know it all by putting herself out there, especially on social media, but as a result of owning her space, she has told the world about the book she has written. She has also created a number of blogs on LinkedIn and runs workshops for other HR professionals. She is now getting noticed by her peers as a person of influence in her profession.

Too many people worry about what others think, comparing themselves to others. This is not the behaviour of someone who owns his or her space. People who own their space come across as confident and everything looks effortless to them. Own your space to become more influential, have more energy, and attract people who align with your values.

Owning your space is both an emotional and a physical state. So how do you do it?

Strike a pose. Stand tall with intent, sit with presence, and have an intentionality that means business. Look up and let your body language tell the world what you're all about.

Develop your self-leadership skills. This is about knowing your intentions, communicating them effectively, being self-aware, being persistent, and above all, believing in yourself.

Decide you belong. You matter and people want to listen to you. Your opinion matters. Never forget that. If you don't decide to belong, others won't see you as someone who matters.

Never compare. Owning your space means you stand on your own two feet. You have a special 'pow' that others don't possess. Remember, you have a unique presence, talent and skills that only you can bring to the party. There will be something that you are world class at, so show the world what that is.

Be more self-aware. Owning your space means you are in touch with and in control of your emotions. You don't react, you respond. Your emotional intelligence is high, so your self-awareness simply reinforces that fact.

Start to own your space immediately. Decide you belong and you matter. The world is waiting for you, so don't let it down.

18. DETACH FROM THE OUTCOME

A lot of elite athletes use NATO. No, not the North Atlantic Treaty Organisation; in this context, the NATO acronym stands for Not Attached To Outcome.

We all have expectations, outcomes we want in our lives. However, these expectations can prevent us from being and performing at our best. When we are attached to an outcome, we are not present to the task at hand. If we are not present to the task at hand, then we are not giving ourselves our best chance to achieve the best outcome.

All sports, especially when they're performed at an elite level, require the athlete to be 'in the moment' to maximise the result. This can be a tough discipline to master, but the results can be powerful.

Some may say it's important to have the end in mind and know exactly what you are aiming for. This is true, but when you are performing or executing a task, you need to be in the moment and focus all your attention on that task. Attaching yourself to the outcome will take some of your focus away from maximising your performance.

So practise like it matters, and perform like it doesn't. When the outcome doesn't matter, the pressure is off. You have no expectations and aren't scared to make a mistake. But when the outcome matters and you think you may only have one chance to succeed, you will be scared to make a mistake. This leads to stress in body and mind, meaning you hinder your performance, which in turn impacts the outcome.

It's easy to see this in a sporting context, where the lines between when you are competing and when you are training are distinct. You are aware when it's competition time and when it's not. But how does NATO work in life, work and business, when it's a constant struggle to be at your best all the time?

Because you're constantly performing, being attached to the outcome and having high expectations will never serve you. When you think about creating a life you desire, you will best serve yourself by training your mind and behaviour so you can be in the moment as much as possible and allow the outcome to look after itself.

How do you do that? It's all about starting from the context of who you are being, which takes us back to the 'Train your thoughts' tip in the previous chapter. We grow up in a society where we learn to want things. Then we work out what actions we need to take to achieve our wants in order to be happy, successful, rich, etc. But when we detach ourselves from the outcome, we approach life the other way round. We decide who we want to be in life, and then we decide what actions we will take to become that person. This allows the result – the riches, the success, the happiness – to look after itself.

Using a sporting example, imagine an athlete training for the Olympics. The athlete who decides to train as a champion, eat like a champion and behave like a champion, even before they win anything, detaches themselves from the outcome and acts from the point of view of the person they want to become.

Decide who you want to be and what actions you are going to take using the NATO method – Not Attached To Outcome.

19. BE LUCKY

'The harder you work, the luckier you get.'
— Gary Player, professional golfer

I believe there is a lot of truth in this quote from Gary Player. Luck is not random.

I am sure you know people who seem to have all the luck and others who just seem to have been born unlucky. But is it possible to be lucky? To a certain extent, yes, it is. In fact, it has been shown to be true through a psychological experiment.

Professor Richard Wiseman of the University of Hertfordshire conducted a study around luck over a ten-year period. The question he asked was, 'Why do some people get all the luck while others never get the breaks they deserve?' He wanted to know why some people always seemed to be in the right place at the right time, while others consistently missed out.

To conduct his study, Professor Wiseman placed advertisements in national newspapers asking for people who felt consistently lucky or unlucky to contact him. Hundreds of ordinary men and women volunteered to take part in the research, and over the years, he interviewed them, monitored their lives and had them take part in experiments.

Professor Wiseman carried out a simple experiment to discover whether luck was due to people's different abilities to spot opportunities. He gave both lucky and unlucky participants a newspaper, asked them to look through it and tell him how many photographs were inside.

Unbeknown to the participants, he had placed a large message halfway through the newspaper, saying, 'Tell the experimenter you have seen this and win $250.' This message took up half of the page and was written in type that was more than two inches high, so it was staring everyone in the face, but the results were extraordinary. Professor Wiseman learnt that the unlucky people tended to miss the advertisement and the lucky people tended to spot it. This is how he explains the effect:

> 'Unlucky people are generally tenser than lucky people, and this anxiety disrupts their ability to notice the unexpected. For example, they look through newspapers determined to find certain types of job advertisements and miss other types of jobs.'

Professor Wiseman's research revealed that lucky people generate good fortune via four principles:

1. They are skilled at creating and noticing opportunities.

2. They make lucky decisions by listening to their intuition.

3. They create self-fulfilling prophesies via positive expectations.

4. They adopt a resilient attitude to transform bad luck into good.

Being entrepreneurial is a lot to do with being in the right place at the right time, saying the right thing to the right people, and looking at the world as a place full of opportunities to innovate and create. Here are Professor Wiseman's four top tips for becoming lucky:

1. Listen to your gut instincts – they are normally right.

2. Be open to new experiences and to breaking out of your normal routine.

3. Spend a few moments each day thinking about things that have gone well.

4. Visualise yourself being lucky when you're preparing for an important meeting or telephone call.

Allowing luck to be on your side is essential to your inner game. Yes, work hard, work smartly, but also expect good things to happen. Expect the right people to turn up when you need them and be the person who everyone else says is lucky. You will know your luck is really just a product of your mindset.

20. BE BRAVE

'There is a great difference between worry and concern. A worried person only sees the problem and a concerned person solves the problem.'
 — *Harold Stephens, author*

One of the single biggest things that stops people doing what they want, being productive and reaching their potential, is fear. There are probably more dreams dashed, opportunities missed, and chances not taken because of fear than anything else. We resist fear, we fight it, and in most cases, we make it bigger than it is. But the popular acronym of FEAR is false evidence appearing real, and fear is exactly that.

We as humans have a habit of making up stories in our heads based on assumptions which then turn into truths. When we look at the hard evidence before us without any assumptions, though, we realise that most of what we are fearful of is simply not true.

Fear is a natural instinct. We need it to survive, but it has evolved into a disabling factor that takes over our thoughts. Fear grows when we have high expectations and attach ourselves to the outcome of those expectations. It doesn't matter how much money we have, how successful we are, or how happy we are, fear will exist in our life, so we need to embrace it. When we start to embrace fear, we can take control of our life.

A method of embracing fear is to lean into it. Take small actions which force you to face the fear as opposed to avoiding it or working around it. Your life expands when you grow outside your comfort zone, and leaning into fear helps you to do this. It also means you start to understand how strong you are, and more importantly, if you face your fears and grow, you will gain more and more evidence to draw upon to prove that you are strong.

Don't let fear overcome you. Look at it, confront it and embrace it. Your inner entrepreneurial spirit can overcome any fear, but you have to be aware of it.

There are three things you can do to embrace fear.

1. Look at the real evidence. List what is true about your fear and list what is not. Then focus on the truth.

2. Be courageous. Fear in action is courage. When you see people who seem to have no fear, it is not true. They feel the fear, but choose to take action anyway. This soon generates a feeling of courage, which in turn gives them more confidence to take more action.

3. Get a coach/mentor. Fear is a result of thinking we are not good enough, or that we need more of something to tackle our fear. Working with a coach or mentor, you can clarify your fears and see that you can face them, right now.

Be brave. Embrace fear. Be courageous. Be vulnerable. All these states of being fall into the same category: they all require you to operate outside your comfort zone. Changing the game is not an easy thing to do, and it is certainly not something you can do if you don't stretch yourself and test how far you can go. It is all about knowing your potential. You won't know how good you are until you test yourself.

Dr David Hawkins talks about the human levels of consciousness in his book *Power vs. Force*. These levels range from shame, guilt, apathy, grief, fear, to desire, anger, pride, courage, neutrality, to willingness, acceptance, reason, love, joy, peace, enlightenment. Dr Hawkins says we can feel all these levels in our lifetime, but depending on our personality, one or two levels will be predominant. The fact that you are reading this book suggests that you are on the higher scale, operating from a level of pride and courage onwards.

Dr Hawkins explains that each level has an energy score. This score indicates the amount of energy we have at our disposal when we operate from that level of consciousness. Fear has a score of 100, and courage has a score of 200, so courage gives us twice the amount of energy to operate from as fear.

When we operate from fear, we make decisions in a panic, which can lead to burnout. We react rather than respond. When we operate from courage, we lean into decisions and have more staying power. If we feel fearful, when we choose to embrace that fear and lean into it, we immediately increase the energy level we have to operate from. This is a scientifically proven fact.

Bravery is stepping into the unknown and doing something we haven't done before. It is also knowing when to say no, staying true to what we believe in the face of what others may expect from us. The people who dare to change the game have to be brave as they are often going against what society and convention expect. They challenge the status quo, they listen to their instinct, and they let go of the past.

The ultimate action of bravery is allowing yourself to be vulnerable. There is strength in your vulnerability. Going back to the levels of consciousness, you have to be courageous to be vulnerable. When you let go of what you know and the things from your past that are holding you back, you become vulnerable. Being vulnerable authentically means you show up without any barriers. You are telling the world that this is who you are, raw and naked.

The only thing that will prevent you from being vulnerable is your ego. The ego wants to protect you from showing weakness, being hurt and giving the impression you cannot cope, but actually, the opposite is true. When you make a change in yourself and show your vulnerability, you are showing the world that you are human; that you are nothing special and have nothing that others don't have. The only difference between you and the people who stay trapped by fear is that you are taking action despite the fear, the risk and the failures you are likely to encounter.

Nothing great has ever happened without people being brave and courageous. You cannot change the game without stepping out of your comfort zone. It's time to take action, now.

There is a simple way to do this. First, you have to choose to do it. By reading this book, you have already taken that choice. A book called *Change Your Game* would not have been picked up by someone operating from a lower level of consciousness. It's not an intelligence issue, it's an awareness issue. The world looks foggy from the lower levels – shame, guilt, apathy, grief, fear – and then it is all about survival.

Now you have chosen to take action, you need to take any action that will move you forward. There are a number of examples of appropriate actions in the third pillar of this book, so choose one and follow it through. By taking that action, you will feel more confident, have more energy and show the world you want to change your game.

21. STAY PRESENT

Stay in the present moment, as that's the only place you can really be. Unfortunately, though, most of us live in the past. We think about what has happened before, things we cannot do anything about, and we use these things to make up a story – a 'truth' that is anything but the truth, but which governs the way we live our lives. The future has not happened yet so it is a complete unknown. Now is all we have.

Signs that you are not staying in the present:

- You worry about things you can't control
- You feel overwhelmed
- You procrastinate
- You don't listen
- You are fearful

When you look at this list, I'm sure you can see that none of these traits are conducive to being a high performer. When you are consciously more present, you are more likely to perform at your best.

There are many benefits of staying in the present moment. To help you understand how staying present can help you perform better, here are some of the benefits.

You feel free. Attaching yourself to the past and the stories you tell yourself about how you should be in your life, you can never be truly free. If you live in the present, you see things as they really are as opposed to how your filters tell you they are from past feelings.

You perform better. Because you are more focused, alert, creative, and aware, you will start to see how powerful you really are.

You build inner peace. You are more centred and feel less anxious.

Your attitude improves. You become grateful for what you have now rather than being focused on what you may have lost in the past or may not achieve in the future.

Being present is a consequence of the actions you take. A lot of the tips in this book will naturally lead you to be more present.

22. DON'T LOOK TO BE PERFECT

The happiest people in the world are not those who have no problems, but those who learn to live with things that are less than perfect.

Depending on your personality type, you may have a tendency to want things to be perfect before you move forward. But when you are in the entrepreneur-ial space and want to make a game-changing impact, you cannot look for perfection.

The reality is that perfection doesn't exist. There is no perfect time to get started. There is no perfect impact you can make. There is no perfect business. There are no perfect circumstances you can wait for. There is no perfect product or service you can create.

Give up on wanting to look perfect as well. This is not a growth mindset. If we turn up, show up as we are, we often believe the world will see all our imperfections and not take us seriously. This is not true. The world wants to see the human being. People know that you are not perfect; none of us are. As we discussed earlier in the chapter, your vulnerability will be your strength.

When you stop striving for perfection, your stress levels will reduce and you will take positive action. Ultimately, you will accept yourself for who you are. You have a choice. Choose who you are.

CASE STUDY – PLANET LEASING

Planet Leasing was one of my first clients. The founders of this company are perfect examples of entrepreneurs not waiting until they were perfect before starting. Their business idea and model was simple, but not common at the time we first worked together.

Darren Nash had been working in the car industry for most of his life when he saw an opportunity to take car leasing to the mass consumer market. Up until then, leasing vehicles had been associated with fleet companies and company cars, not the general public.

In 2007, Darren approached Gary Rose with the concept of starting a car leasing company for the consumer market. At the start, all they had was a phone and a list of people who owned cars. No website, no testimonials, just a belief that the market was ready to have a brand new car without needing to own it.

I have worked with Darren and Gary on and off for the last ten years on sales and business strategy. Their company, Planet Leasing, now has a team of sales professionals in three locations around the country and is known as one of the UK's leading vehicle leasing brokers.

Five things you can do to let go of being perfect.

1. Accept who you are. You cannot be anyone but yourself. Your imperfections make you perfectly you, because no one else has the same imperfections.

2. Keep it simple. Don't do too much. Multi-tasking is a fallacy; you will actually get nothing done by multi-tasking. Keeping it simple will ensure you get more done.

3. Have perspective. This is a great leveller. Not everything is as bad as it seems, nor is everything as good as it seems. Look at yourself from a third person perspective. Think of someone you really respect – how would they see the world from your eyes? What would they see? What are you not allowing yourself to see?

4. Look at the big picture. Perfectionists get bogged down in the detail. Details matter in some cases, but not all. Is what you've already got good enough? Will the detail you are focusing on today matter tomorrow?

5. Stop procrastinating. We procrastinate because we have no plan, no clear direction, or are fearful of the result. When you realise this and take action in the face of it, you will see results that will likely surprise you, and this will give you the energy to carry on. Procrastination steals your time while you look for the perfect solution. There isn't one.

The good news is that no one expects you to be perfect. In fact, if you seem to be perfect, people think there must be something wrong, that you're too good to be true. Give yourself a break from trying to be perfect and just be the authentic you. That is what the world is waiting to see.

Now you know that perfection is not possible, there is no need to wait any longer. It's time to make a game plan.

PILLAR TWO

THE GAME PLAN

Have A Life Plan

23. MAKE YOUR ACTIONS MIRROR YOUR WISHES

Do you have things you wish for? Have any of your wishes come true? Did your actions mirror your wishes?

I have not yet met a person who does not want success, a good life and freedom to do what they want to do. The problem is, these wishes often don't mirror the actions they take.

When you have big wishes, things that you want to do and achieve, there is no free lunch. There is a price you have to pay. That price is action – action that can be uncomfortable.

Life is littered with unfulfilled goals because no action was taken. Or if action was taken, it was the wrong action. No, let me rephrase that: it was action which was not followed through.

Nothing happens without action. Taking actions that align with your wishes is life changing, and in order to take this action, you need a life plan that is clear, flexible and congruent with your values.

Let's play a little game here. Take a pen and paper or start a document on your favourite device and list your top five wishes. Wishes are different to goals in this context in that they are less specific and they relate to the big picture, but they must still be aligned to your values.

Looking at your wishes, list specific goals that you could set to make them come true. These goals need to be SMART – specific, measurable, attainable, realistic and timed.

Once you have your SMART goals, list three actions you can take for each goal and think about the actions. For example, if you wish you could help more people, maybe you will set a goal of writing a book. The first major action would be to plan the book or come up with a title, but I want you to list the smallest actions you will take. Before you plan the book or come up with the title, you may look at some websites, research courses on how to write a book, or ask other authors to recommend a writing coach. The preparatory actions are as important as the main actions you will take around that goal.

Making these lists will likely boost your confidence. By completing the small tasks you have set yourself around your goal, you will feel like you are progressing. You will see how much you can get done towards a goal that may have seemed unachievable at the start. This will give you new perspectives on what you can achieve.

Make these actions as small as possible (see 'Micro goals' in the 'Good Habits' chapter) and see how much you can get done. Achieving micro goals consistently will help make your wishes come true.

24. GET GOOD ONLINE

In 1990, a momentous thing happened. This was the year when what we now know as the internet became recognisable. The internet was actually invented in 1983, but it wasn't until Tim Berners-Lee invented the World Wide Web, allowing the world to be connected through telephone lines and later a Wi-Fi network, that it took on the form we know today.

As of 2016, around 40% of the world's population had an internet connection. In 1995, it was less than 1%. Based on this, it doesn't take a genius to work out that within another twenty years, the majority of the world will be connected online. So to be good online is no longer an option, it is a necessity.

What does being good online mean? The generations who have been born into a world where having Wi-Fi is as normal as having Ready Brek or tomato ketchup don't distinguish between being offline and being online. The two overlap and merge so much that they cannot be distinguished.

This is both good and bad. It's good from the point of view that it's becoming second nature for people to be online, but it's bad from the point of view that there are some behaviours online that are less than desirable.

To get good online is to understand the power of your personal brand, the impact of social networks, and the speed at which content is communicated. Zero Moment of Truth (ZMOT) is a study done by Google that looks at the behaviour of people online, when and how they research information, and the decisions they make. If you want to be seen online in a favourable way, I would recommend you take a look at this study as it is important you understand how people behave online and how to position your personal brand accordingly.

I will discuss ZMOT more in the next chapter.

25. EMBRACE SOCIAL MEDIA

I would guess that you use social media in some capacity. If you use social media regularly, this section will help you to ensure you are really embracing it.

Like it or not, social media is here to stay. In fact, it's now part of the fabric of our society. Social media can affect every occasion and incident in our life – sports events are tweeted, celebrations are shared on Facebook, we are telling people about our day in Snapchat. To be entrepreneurial is to be curious, adapt to the current trends, be creative, and spot opportunities. Social media caters for all these traits in abundance.

Many mistakenly think that social media is a marketing and broadcasting tool. Those who use it to its maximum realise it is an engagement platform and a place to connect with people. When you make this mindset shift, what you may now see as a stream of random comments will turn into conversations and insights to engage with.

Embrace the opportunity to connect with people around the world. Take part in conversations on subjects close to your heart with people you have never met and create opportunities with partners who love what you do. These are just a couple of the many benefits of embracing social media.

Three actions you can take to shift your mindset on social media are:

1. Earn the right to broadcast. Before you start to post on social media, increase your authority and credibility by listening to, acknowledging and connecting with people on the platforms you intend to use.

If we are all broadcasting on social, who is listening? Would you go to a social event and just talk without engaging or listening first? No, neither would I. So why do that on social media? Think of social media as one big cocktail party where there are conversations happening all over the place, and you can listen and contribute to these conversations any time you want.

2. Acknowledge and connect with others. It is so easy to acknowledge what people say and do on social, and this has numerous benefits. One, it makes them feel good; two, it makes you look good; and three, their connections will notice you as well and may connect with you. The ongoing benefit of this is that you start to build relationships with random people that may lead to opportunities, all because you turned up and noticed others.

3. Believe your voice is worth hearing. Social media amplifies your voice to the world without costing you anything. Unleashing your entrepreneurial spirit means you believe in what you have to say and that others will want to hear it. Engage in Facebook groups, take part in Twitter chats, post images on Instagram, and document your insights in Snapchat. All of these platforms, as well as many others, amplify your voice.

Out of every ten people on social media, only two or three are using it to its full potential, so embracing it gives you an advantage. Change the way you look at social media and social media will change the way it works for you.

26. SPEAK LIKE A KING

Speaking in public is a skill that I believe needs to be taught from a young age. Children are naturally expressive, and if we nurture these natural skills, we will help them in many areas of their lives as they grow up.

When you communicate effectively, especially when you speak in public, it can make all the difference. It naturally builds confidence and it is a skill that you can use for the rest of your life.

By nature, we are lazy listeners. We want information coming to us that is not only easily digestible, but easy to understand. It is therefore your responsibility to speak like a king. But what does that mean? It means that you present with such clarity that the way you are doing it is not even noticeable. Your audience will just hear your message.

Speaking in public comes naturally to some people, but fills most with fear. In fact, public speaking is one of the top three fears for a lot of people. But if you overcome this fear, you open up a multitude of doors. The fears around public speaking are, like most fears, never actually well founded.

The fears associated with public speaking include a fear of being judged, looking stupid, forgetting words, sounding boring, the audience knowing more than we do, and feeling like we must know it all. But think about when you are listening to someone else – do you think any of these things about them? It's far more likely that you will want them to do well and want to know their take on a subject. You may also feel for them if something does go wrong and relate to them far more because they then appear human and authentic.

There are some key things to remember when you are speaking in public. People mostly remember how you made them feel, not what you said. You can be presenting the best and most useful content ever, but if it's not communicated in a compelling and engaging manner, your message will be lost.

Don't fall into the trap of thinking you need to know everything about your subject area. You don't. What people want to know is your take on a subject. Focus on one thing you want the audience to get and stick to that. Your goal when you speak in public is to connect with the audience. When you have connected with the audience, their mindset will change. They will want to hear what you have to say because they will believe in you.

The next thing to remember is to be as authentic as possible. Don't try to copy someone else's style and delivery. It is tempting to copy the way someone else speaks if you love their style and how they connect with the audience, but the likelihood is that what works for them won't work for you. Develop your own style and speak from the heart.

Plan Your Business

27. CREATE SOMETHING BIGGER THAN YOU

A few years back, I embarked on a personal development course run by Landmark Education. I had known about this course for many years, but decided to do it at a time when things were challenging for me in both my personal and business life. Like with so many things, I wish I had done the course earlier in my life, but hindsight is a great thing.

The course that allowed me to think about the world as a massive opportunity was the 'Self Expression and Leadership Program' (SELP). The premise of this course is that you cannot be truly self-expressed or be a leader without creating something bigger than what you believe is possible. If you just participate in activities that serve your lifestyle and ensure you are OK, then you will never realise your full potential.

In the SELP, the participants create a project to serve the communities they are already part of. For me at the time, this was family and friends, my cricket club, the entrepreneurs' and personal development world, and the schools I did work in.

When I worked in the corporate world, it was pretty much dog eat dog. We all did what we needed to do to get ahead without worrying about others. I was caught in this trap for seventeen years. My thinking had to change.

Doing the SELP took my thinking to another level. This meant I could create things that went beyond my own success. It was about making an impact.

Think about a project so big that it can only become a reality if you enrol others into your vision. When you do this, you stop thinking about what you can or cannot do, and start to think about the impact the project will make on other people's lives if it becomes a reality.

The project I created was an event called 'Wanna Be an Entrepreneur?' This is an extravaganza involving over 300 sixth formers listening to entrepreneurs talking about how to create the life they desire. To date, I have already run three of these extravaganzas.

Creating this project has given me access to a new way of thinking to achieve things I didn't believe were possible before.

CASE STUDY – GRANDEUR AND LOVE

Grandeur and Love is a high-end matchmaking company looking to teach true connection to help clients find their life partner. It is a perfect example of how looking at the bigger picture and collaborating with others can create win-wins.

In simple terms, the bigger picture for Grandeur and Love is to take a matchmaking service to a new level, understanding that just because some people may want to date, it doesn't mean they are ready. The company has created a whole coaching service that looks at the clients' mindset, style and ambitions.

In order to help clients with style, Grandeur and Love found a perfect collaboration with image consultants and personal style specialists, House of Colour. The two companies offer different services to the same target market. House of Colour loved the idea and have created a package for Grandeur and Love.

Grandeur and Love have created a style package which includes an image consultation, plus mentoring around the dos and don'ts of a first date and how to receive and give compliments that make their clients and their dates feel good. Looking at the bigger picture beyond matchmaking, Grandeur and Love found a win-win-win – a win for the clients, a win for House of Colour, and a win for Grandeur and Love itself.

As we can see from this case study, the secret to collaboration is to look for partners whose products or services complement yours without the fear of overlap.

Do you need big thinking to create a big project, or can starting a big project lead to big thinking? For me, it was conceiving the project that forced me to think and act in new ways.

When it comes to big thinking, it doesn't get much bigger than Elon Musk. Launching Tesla Motors for him wasn't about making money; he'd already sold PayPal and Zip2 for millions, which he then poured into Tesla. He was thinking of a project so much bigger than himself. He wanted to make transport environmentally friendly, so invested his money in the technology of electric motors. He is so passionate about this project that his technology is available to other transport manufacturers because he knows Tesla alone cannot change the whole industry.

What could you create that is bigger than you? What gets you going? What makes you angry? Start with what is in your heart.

28. UNDERSTAND HOW YOUR MARKET THINKS

Whether you are running your own business or you work for someone else, you need to understand how your market thinks. If you are looking to make a game-changing impact, you need to understand how your market thinks. Any entrepreneur or business-person must understand their audience.

Why is understanding your market so important? The world is full of people who are making a game-changing impact. One of the main differences between them and those who don't make an impact is the successful game changers are empathic. They all understand their audience.

With social media, artificial intelligence, message bots, various lookalike audience statistics, and different tools to collect audience data, the opportunities to understand your audience are vast.

CASE STUDY - CAR-NECT AUTO GROUP

Car-nect Auto Group on the surface is a group of car mechanics. It offers MOTs, servicing, repairs - all the things you would expect car mechanics to provide.

When I worked with the group's owners, I realised they wanted to understand how their market thinks so they could position Car-nect Auto Group above its competitors. We started with why they do what they do, and then worked on how they could deliver on this. The company's 'why' was to provide manufacturer-level service at an affordable price; its 'what' was to be the best main dealer alternative.

Once the owners knew what their company's differential was, it was time to understand what their target market thought. Through customer surveys, campaigns and feedback from third party data, they discovered that many customers didn't trust a main dealer alternative to offer top-level service at a low price. They were unsure if using an alternative would mean their warranty would become invalid and whether the main dealer alternative would be using genuine parts.

Having collected this data, we redeveloped the company's marketing and communications towards reassuring the prospects that their fears were unfounded, all the while informing them of the types of services Car-nect were offering. This, along with redesigning the website and where the company marketed, started to gain more clients and encourage existing customers to come back.

The marketplace is much more savvy nowadays. People won't be influenced by messages being pushed in their faces. They know what they want, they know what they like, and they know what they are going to respond to.

As I mentioned in the previous chapter, in 2012, Google wrote a paper called 'Zero Moment of Truth' (ZMOT). This paper talks about how the internet has changed the buying habits of consumers and the way they are influenced by the messages they are exposed to second by second. ZMOT gives us an insight into when people actually take action and make a purchase.

When you understand how your market thinks and behaves, you can save a lot of time and money. Your target customers will have different attitudes based on where they are in the market relative to your product or service. These attitudes result in different behaviours:

- 50% of the market cannot see the value you offer so they are not loyal to you. All they are looking for is a freebie. This is the market you need to *stimulate*

- 40% of prospects are looking for their next solution. This market needs you to *educate* them

- 7% of the market gets you, but lacks the confidence to make a decision. They want your offering, but not yet. These are the prospects who need a *consultation*

- 3% of the market gets you and wants your offering. These are your clients and they want to be *served*

Most people communicate to prospects like they are all part of the 3% or 7%, but as you can see, 90% of the marketplace needs either stimulation or education. That is one reason why ZMOT's work is so important.

You can find out more about ZMOT at:

www.thinkwithgoogle.com/intl/en-gb/marketing-resources/data-measurement/2012-zmot-handbook

29. UNDERSTAND HOW TO PIVOT

You may well have heard the phrase 'Never give up'. But what does this really mean?

It means that if you want something badly enough, you have to work for it constantly, however tough it gets. Nothing worthwhile ever comes easily.

However, there may come a time in business when you have to re-evaluate where you are, what you are doing, where you are going, and what you want to achieve. This means you may have to pivot.

Pivoting is not giving up; it's being pragmatic. It is being smart and courageous to ensure you reach the right outcome, and it can sometimes be scary. Those who understand how to pivot are real game changers. They see something that others don't, they trust their instincts and they take action.

Here are seven things you can do to ensure you pivot properly:

1. Go back to your vision. Pivoting is about taking a different path, not changing the destination. What in your current plan is not aligned with the vision?

2. List what doesn't feel right. This could include people, marketing strategies, or the makeup of your product or service. Involve your team in the discussion if you have one. If not, find a coach or mentor who can help you look objectively at your project/business.

3. Take a step back. Don't rush. Take your time to see what is really going wrong. Even when you think you know what you're doing, take a step back, breathe, and be totally clear about it in your mind.

4. Develop a new plan. If you have one, share this process with your team. Can they see what you see? Does this new path feel to them like a better way to meet your vision?

5. Ditch the old path. Don't look back. Yes, learn from your old path, but don't become anchored to it. You want your new path to your vision to be clear.

6. Define the new metrics. How are you going to ensure the new plan is right? Have KPIs in place so you can see how the pivot is working.

7. Be prepared to pivot again. Don't assume your first pivot will work. Often it won't, so test and measure, then test and measure some more. If truth be told, you are always testing and measuring when you are running a business, especially when it is game changing.

Don't be afraid to change paths and pivot; it's part of the nature of changing the game. If we knew what to do from the start, we would all be doing what we love. But only a select few do.

Understanding when to pivot is as key as the process of pivoting itself. Here are some of the common signs:

- Your plan doesn't feel right
- The market is not responding as you want it to
- You aren't getting short-term results
- People you respect are not seeing it
- You have a lot of groundhog days

This is where a good coach or mentor can really help. They will see what you can't see, they will be truthful and they will challenge you.

When you know you have to pivot, don't do it alone. Surround yourself with people who get you, understand you, will challenge you and have your best interests at heart.

30. CREATE WEALTH, NOT INCOME

One of the key learnings from my ten years as an entrepreneur is the difference between creating wealth and creating income.

Before my entrepreneurial life started, I had a career as a psychology lecturer and then as a sales director. Both were salaried positions. I had no other income. Leaving the supposed 'security' of a job meant that I was in charge of creating my own wealth as well as generating an income.

A mindset you need to adopt is one of creating wealth, not just an income. When you think of creating income, you're thinking of the short term, ensuring you cover the basics and hoping that you have some money left for a rainy day. This is not the mindset of someone who is investing in him- or herself.

Wealth is not just about money, it is about having an abundance mindset. One event which occurred in 2006 stands out for me; I can remember it like it happened yesterday.

I was at a seminar about investing in property. At one point during the presentation, the picture of two reality TV 'stars' flashed up on the screen. The speaker asked the audience how many of us recognised these people. There were about 200 people in the audience, and I was among the 75% who put their hands up.

The speaker then went on to tell us that if we had our hands up, we were consumers of time rather than investors of time, and this attitude would need to change if we were to be successful in creating wealth. Watching TV (especially trash TV) and reading or watching the news was consuming my time, so how could I say I was investing my time to better my future and myself?

This hit me hard. I looked at my whole life, where I was consuming and where I was investing, and I am ashamed to admit that a lot of my life at that point was about consuming.

Things changed as soon as I started my own business.

When you think about creating wealth, both in monetary terms and life terms, you need to look at where to invest in yourself. From a financial point of view, you have to think about multiple streams of income. Developing assets, in both business and life, requires a shift in mindset from what you can consume to what you can invest in.

The key learning here is that if you have one source of income, you are not creating wealth. Are you using your income to invest in assets that will give you a return on your investment? Shifting the way you invest in yourself will help you create monetary wealth.

There are lots of ways to invest your time more productively, many of which are listed in this book. For me, the top five are:

- Meditate
- Attend seminars and workshops that expand your thinking
- Meet new people who are playing a bigger game than you
- Exercise
- Keep a journal

There is a great saying, 'Wealth is what is left in your life when you take away all the things money cannot buy.' Commit to making your wealth list as long as possible.

Believe In Your Brand

31. DEVELOP YOUR TRIBE

One of the first things I noticed that game changers were doing was building their community, their audience, their tribe *before* they created and sold a product or service to them. Seth Godin, the world famous marketer, talks about the importance of doing this in his book *Tribes,* written back in 2011, well ahead of its time.

Creating a tribe of loyal followers is not about becoming a celebrity. It is not about selling stuff, manipulating people or having to persuade them to follow you. Developing your tribe is about enrolling people into what you believe is possible in the world. It is about becoming someone of note who people respect, admire and want to be around. It's about taking a position, communicating that position, and then inviting people to join you if they believe in what you are saying. People join, for their own reasons, to be part of something that makes them feel good because your values resonate with theirs.

Nothing great has ever been achieved by one man or woman. It often takes one man or woman to make a start, to take a position, to speak first, but after that, they will need other people around them. They will need people who believe in the same things as they do and support them for that reason.

With technology and social media, it is so easy to develop your tribe.

Claire Perry-Louise, who is an expert in building communities that engage, explains it like this:

> 'I think it is essential to find your own tribe and community because if you surround yourselves with the right people then not only will you thrive and grow, but so will the people around you.
>
> 'I believe that we pass through different cycles in society. In the past we lived in small communities, we used the local services in that community, and word of mouth and

referrals gave us the tools to make decisions as to which [*companies*] we should do business with. The invention of the car, train, and plane, the internet etc has broken these localised community ties and moved us into another era. We have been able to purchase according to price not by referral, we are not tied to locality, and we have just gone for the cheapest and quickest [*solutions to our problems*].

'Then came social media, which started to connect us all again. As part of this, we started to look to others for recommendations and returned to doing business with those who created communities for us to be a part of, for example, Apple and Amazon. We are tired of being followed around on our devices by adverts, tricked into giving our email address and stuck in funnels. We have information overload. We stopped opening our emails. What we want now is to return to the community, be nurtured and receive real value. We want to feel valued and not just be a number. As employees, we are actively searching out the companies with the best cultures.

'Times are changing and as leaders, we need to now address culture and community in our organisations.'

The times we live in demand that we develop our tribe. People are waiting for us to change the game so they can live the life they desire. Changing the game is about seeing the big picture. We cannot do that without developing our tribe.

The great thing about developing our tribe is that it is not a linear process; it is exponential. Developing our tribe is about starting a movement, bringing people together to change the world in a positive way.

A great TED video by Derek Sivers about how to start a movement explains this perfectly. You can watch it here: www.youtube.com/watch?v=V74AxCqOTvg. In it, one man is dancing enthusiastically on a crowded hillside. Initially, people are just looking at him, thinking he is weird, but a few minutes later, one person joins him to dance. This is the first follower. The first follower is crucial as they give others confidence to join the party.

When the second follower joins, momentum kicks in. Now the leader's job is to maintain the space and allow people to join for their own reasons.

The great part about developing your tribe is that it is fun and exciting. The world needs people like you to lead, ready to change the game.

Develop your tribe by standing up for something you value. It doesn't matter how big or small it is, as long as it resonates with you. Marketers understand their target audience; they know the audience's dislikes, likes, ages, jobs, economic statuses, and relationship statuses. Leaders who develop tribes focus on what they stand for, and then the market finds them.

Developing a tribe is a process that doesn't necessarily have an end goal. Instead it has milestones to hit:

Have a clear purpose. People have to know what you stand for and relate to it.

Keep it small. A tribe starts with one person, then two. As the 'How to Start a Movement' TED talk demonstrates, you need to focus on attracting two or three people who are as invested in your purpose as you are, so don't worry if your tribe stays relatively small for a period of time. Grow too big too soon and you will risk making people feel as if they are not a valued part of the crowd. This means you won't truly connect with them.

Use social media. You cannot grow your tribe without it, but there are strategies and tactics involved – too many to list here. When you are clear on your purpose, you will be clear on what platforms to use.

Stay personal. Don't hide behind a brand, be the brand. This doesn't mean you don't have to give your brand a name and a great look, but ensure it is indistinguishable from your personal values and ethos.

Be current. People like to belong to something that is innovative. There is nothing new in the world, but your take on anything will be unique. The duty of a game-changing leader is to look at the world in a way that others will relate to, but don't have the vision and purpose to create.

Create anticipation. Drip feed what you stand for to the crowd. Entice people with what they can look forward to. The best way to do this is through content marketing, events and launches. When your tribe is looking forward to something tangible that they want to be a part of, you create real anticipation and momentum.

Support your tribe. As you develop your tribe, your job as the leader is to support it. The tribe wants leaders to lead, empower and be present, so be available to them, especially in the early stages.

32. SOLVE A PROBLEM

When we are young and deciding on our future, we are often asked, 'What do you want to do?' There is enormous pressure on us to know what we want to do with the rest of our lives. Depending on how old you are now, you may still be working this out.

A better question to ask ourselves when we are working out what we want to do would be, 'What problem do I want to solve?' It doesn't matter how intelligent we think we are, what qualifications we have, what experience we have, we all have it within us to solve a problem.

There are two universal truths:

- There will always be a problem to be solved in the world
- Nothing is unsolvable – I say this with confidence because history has shown it to be true

Some of the greatest ideas, movements, businesses and memorable moments have come about as a result of a game changer focusing on solving a problem. Richard Branson famously came up with the idea of launching Virgin Airlines after an unpleasant experience of booking a flight from London to New York. Steve Jobs wanted to create a computer that allowed people to solve their own problems while having a great user experience, and so the Mac was born. The Wright brothers had the crazy idea of solving the problem of humans being unable to fly and the first manned flight occurred.

What problem exists in the world that you think needs an alternative solution?

With the advancement of technology, you can now solve problems with resources that didn't exist five years ago. Game changing is all about solving problems, so start with the problem in mind and work backwards. Essentially, reverse engineer the problem.

Here are some useful questions to ask yourself when you're looking for a problem to solve:

- What is a constant frustration that you would like an alternative solution to?

- When you have found a solution to the problem, what would work better? Don't think about how you are going to solve it, think about what you want life to look like when you have done it.

- What would you like to see work better?

Think about the problem you want to solve in a big way, but take small incremental actions towards solving it. Don't make the problem about you, make it bigger than you. Think about the benefits to others when you do solve this problem. If you make it about you, your own limitations, doubts and fears will kick in. The problem will not care what you believe; it will only be sorted out by the solution.

There is a part of the brain called the reticular activating system (RAS). The RAS is the switch that turns on your perceptions of ideas and data, meaning it will seek out the things you focus on. It will only find solutions based on what you focus on, so make sure the problem you want to solve takes centre stage in your mind.

The problem you have chosen won't be easy to solve. If it were, it would already have been solved, so you need to be persistent in your search for a solution. Don't overcomplicate the solution by doing too many things at once, and don't take massive steps to solve the problem quickly. Rome was not built in a day. Small steps each day will keep your enthusiasm up and allow you to see progress. Stay true to yourself and know the solution to the problem is what the world needs.

What was unachievable ten years ago that is achievable now? One obvious answer is mobile technology. In our pockets, we can carry a phone, calculator, TV, movie maker, camera, typewriter, alarm clock, along with facilities to play music, check email, study courses, access maps, book holidays, display photos – the list goes on. Things evolve and game changers make things happen.

To be a game changer, you have to solve a problem that is bigger than you. When you think about the problem you want to solve, think about pain points that people currently have. True game changers see problems as opportunities, and they see these opportunities before anyone else does. The opportunity a game changer sees may not even be regarded as a problem by most people.

When Bill Gates said he wanted every home to have a PC, people didn't see that as a problem that needed to be solved. But now we can see why every home does need a home computer, and the reliance we put on them.

When Uber formed, people weren't wishing there was a better way to book a taxi. Uber saw an opportunity, a gap in the market, and solved a problem that many did not even realise existed. At the time of writing, Uber has had its Transport for London licence revoked. There is uproar; people are complaining that they will now not be able to use a service that solved the problem of getting a ride through their phones at a reasonable cost.

The problem you solve could pivot from an existing solution, like Airbnb, for example. No one was looking to hire other people's private rooms and houses when Airbnb first came up with the idea, but now this solution has enabled a brand new service for both consumer and seller.

My journey from academic to corporate junkie to running my own business was all about solving new problems along the way. This book is part of my next big solution – creating a society that thinks in an entrepreneurial way to create a life each person desires. When I first came up with this idea, I didn't know how I was going to do it. All I knew was that it was my mission.

What was really liberating was that as soon as I became clear on my mission, my life became centred on achieving it. I have run three 'Wanna Be an Entrepreneur?' extravaganzas for sixth formers, launched a platform called www.EnSpirit.Global, which has 100 people contributing content every month, run events and seminars teaching entrepreneurial thinking, and created the jewel that is the Global Impact Network.

Make it about others; you are just the facilitator. If you bring the problem to life and find the new solution, others will say, 'Wow, why didn't I think of that?' Make people stand up and take notice. If the problem you are looking at only takes a few months to solve, it is not big enough. Solve something that will take time, but ensure the incremental stages make an impact as well.

The biggest issue with trying to solve a problem is that there is no road map. You have to make it up as you go along. You will make errors, you will fail, you will take two steps forward and three steps back sometimes, but keep the end goal in mind and you will get there.

33. CREATE A PERSONAL BRAND

There is no getting away from it, if you want to change the game, you have to have a personal brand – preferably a brand that you have intentionally created. Your brand is all about others understanding what you stand for.

It would be useful here to clarify what creating a brand means. A brand in the context of a product or service is the image the consumers have in their heads when they think of that product. For example, Virgin brings customer focus, fun, modern products and services to mind. Apple brings innovation, customer-centred experiences and modern technology to mind.

For your personal brand, what do you want it to make people think of? If you don't take charge of your brand message, the image you are portraying could be the wrong one. It needs to be all about what you stand for to ensure the right people gravitate towards you.

This is what creating your personal brand will do for you:

- You will become clear about what you want to do

- You will attract the right people to you

- Opportunities that were not previously available will become available to you

- You will become more focused on your activity

- You will create your own niche that others can identify with

Now you know what creating your personal brand will do for you, how do you create it? The simple answer is personal assets.

Today we are so fortunate to have free or low-cost applications and services that allow us to create personal assets. Here are three of the best ways to create your personal brand:

1. Social media. Social media platforms are efficient, fast, cheap and powerful ways to create your person brand. Twitter, Facebook, Instagram, LinkedIn, YouTube are all platforms that allow you to create a profile and position yourself for free. If you search for me, Baiju Solanki, on any of these platforms, you will see that I have created a brand consistent with my mission – helping you to be the best version of you and change the game in your life and business.

Other platforms that will enhance your brand are Snapchat and Pinterest, depending on the market you want to influence.

2. Content. It doesn't matter what kind of business you are in, content is crucial. People want to consume good quality content, and in the first instance, they want it to be free content.

Content can come in many forms: written, audio, video, images, and in many formats: books, Facebook lives, Instagram stories, infographics, LinkedIn articles, Twitter updates. Whatever the form or format, content is an asset that will create and develop your personal brand.

3. Partners. In the past, getting ahead was all about knowing and beating your competition. Now it's all about creating partnerships and collaborations.

The mindset of abundance allows you to believe there is enough to go round for everyone and that we can all have what we want, as long as we help enough people get what they want. When we collaborate, we are looking at creating win-win-win situations just like the Grandeur and Love case study in the 'Create something bigger than you' section.

The easiest way to change the game is to use your personal brand to create leverage for you and your business. This will make it easier for the market to come to you.

Expand Your Success

34. MASTER NETWORKING

If you really want to change the game, networking is essential. When you master your relationships with people around you, that's when your world will change.

Mastering the way you connect with people is a skill. We often mistake networking with meeting people and telling them what we do in the hope they may want to know more about us and buy our services or products. There are many reasons to network. It doesn't matter whether you run your own business, work for someone else, or are looking to make connections outside a business setting, the methodology and your mindset towards networking should not alter.

Why is networking so important in the context of developing your entrepreneurial thinking? The fundamental reason to network is to build relationships. Where those relationships lead can be very exciting. We are not taught in school the importance of business relationships and mastering how we connect with others, which is a shame. When we have great connections and relationships with people doors open, opportunities increase, and our influence becomes greater than ever.

Networking has changed enormously over the last four to five years, and this is where strategy comes into play. It's a skill we can acquire.

CASE STUDY – SOUTHEND PEERS

One of the first things I realised when I started my own business was that it is whom you know and not what you know that is key to business success. I started networking one month into my entrepreneurial journey and it was one of the best decisions I've ever made.

I went to many groups. One group that I led for a couple of years was Southend Peers, a group of twenty-five to thirty business owners who got together one morning a week to support, inspire and help generate business for each other. As the chairman, it was my responsibility to maximise the opportunities for all the business owners to get business from the group.

There were three main things I introduced:

1. Pitching each other's business – each member would pitch someone else's business, which enabled them to see it from a different perspective.

2. Solutions round table – we got into groups of three, and one member of each group talked about a challenge in their business. The other two members then provided their solutions.

3. Masterclasses – every member knew something that the others would benefit from, so each month one member was given the opportunity to offer a business solution to the group.

Networking isn't just about meeting and telling people what you do, it is about helping people grow as businesses and individuals.

There are five core reasons why networking in some form or other needs to be a part of your regular activities.

1. You develop friends with benefits. No, not that kind! When you go networking, there is a high probability you will meet likeminded people. If you are meeting in a work or business context, everyone will have a business mindset. If you network from a personal context, you are likely to be surrounded by people who want to socialise and have fun.

From a business point of view, you come together in a networking situation not to make friends, but to build relationships. However, the natural consequence will be that you will make some great friends. When you continue to build those relationships, anything can happen. You may find new business associates or long-term advocates. Clients and suppliers will then come to you.

Many people when they go networking make the mistake of going from the point of view of trying to find business. Would you do business with anyone you didn't like? I certainly wouldn't. When you're networking, go to build relationships, not business. That will follow naturally.

2. You will discover unplanned opportunities. Sometimes unplanned opportunities are gold. There is so much information out there about planning, setting goals and strategy, which is all relevant. Sometimes, though, it's the opportunities that come from left field that provide the greatest return on investment.

When you start a network, you don't know whom you are going to meet. You also don't know how other people will see you. Don't be surprised to find out that you are exactly the kind of person someone else needs to work with. And working with them may allow you to fulfil your dreams.

3. You build your influence. One of the biggest reasons I go networking is to build my influence, not only in terms of the work I do, but also in terms of the impact I want to make in the world. Whatever the reasons are that you go networking, in order for you to truly change your game, you have to show evidence that you are serious about doing so. Networking is a fantastic way to do that.

4. You create advocates. It is easy to go to a networking event with a selfish purpose, but if you go with an open mind and understand the power of advocacy, massive opportunities and friendships can open up. An advocacy mindset means you listen and relate to people in a different way. You're not looking for what you can get for yourself, you are looking out for others. This is powerful because one good deed often leads to another and they start to look out for you.

5. You gain insights. Google doesn't know everything. When you look at people for who they are and what experiences they bring to a situation rather than what they do, the insights and knowledge you gain can be invaluable. Once you start to build relationships and connect more regularly, you will see the person behind the label.

When I started networking properly over ten years ago, I was told that my influence would be directly proportional to my network. The more likeminded people you know, the greater your opportunities to create wealth will be.

35. INNOVATE

If you are not innovating, you are not just standing still, you are moving backwards. The speed of change is so fast now that innovation is essential for any business, especially when you are pursuing a life you desire.

What is innovation? Innovation is the process of taking an idea and creating a service or product of value. When you are innovating in relation to your life, you are taking action to improve your living conditions.

How important is innovation if you want to change the game? Like many of the things we have talked about in this book, it is essential.

The word innovation frightens some people off. They think innovation needs lots of resources, knowledge and insights into how to make things happen. Not true. Innovation is a thought process that turns into tangible action. It builds relationships in new ways, develops new ways of thinking, encourages people to take risks, opens up new markets, and gives value to people's ideas.

When you innovate, you don't stand still. You stand out; you are seen as someone who is forward thinking; you are someone who says, 'Look, I can see a different world and a different way of doing things.'

CASE STUDY - LIBERTY HYGIENE

Scott Marshall is the founder and CEO of Liberty Hygiene, a washroom hygiene and waste removal company. Prior to staring the company in 2006, Scott used to work for another well-known washroom services provider. At the back of his mind, he always knew he could do it better.

One common theme in the industry was the contracts the customers would be tied into. They were lengthy and often complicated with many terms and conditions, meaning they were almost impossible to get out of. Scott made the radical decision to have no contract at all. All his customers were free to cancel at any time without giving a reason.

On the surface, this was high risk. When a customer came on board, all the equipment had to be installed upfront at Liberty's expense. Liberty was completely reliant on the quality of the service it provided and ensuring this continued to retain its customers and make a profit.

Ten years on, this small innovation has made Liberty a main player in the washroom services market, securing clients such as Claridge's, Windsor Castle, The Gherkin and Lloyds of London, to name but a few.

When you innovate, what are the practical elements? These are relevant whether you are looking to innovate in a business context or changing areas of your life.

1. Observe. Really look at what is happening in the world and see what is changing. How are people talking? What are they saying?

2. Ask questions. If you're innovating in a business context, ask your customers what they want. What do they want to be solved? What do they feel they need? In life, if you want to make innovative changes, ask someone who has what you want what they did. Success leaves clues.

3. Collaborate. You have something that someone else will want, and you will want what someone else has. Collaboration is the new competition. We have an abundance of resources; there are plenty to go around. When we collaborate, it is the ultimate innovation.

The thing about innovation is that it doesn't have to be radical. As the Liberty Hygiene case study demonstrates, one small change can make a massive difference to the way your product or service is viewed.

36. EXPAND YOUR DREAM

If you are going to have a dream, you may as well have a big dream. What is really surprising, though, is that many people don't. Before we move on, I want to look at why this is.

When we are growing up, the world is our oyster. Anything is possible. Ask a child what they want to do and all sorts of creative thoughts will come out of their mouths.

Then we grow up, and in the process, society, family and friends persuade us to compress our dreams into what they feel is possible. But what is possible? Often we answer this question with a number of conditions attached.

What is possible...

- with my perceived skill level?
- with the resources I have?
- with the money I earn?
- with the talent I have?
- with the people I know?
- with the qualifications I possess?
- based on where I live?
- in the time I have available?
- with the confidence I have?
- with the responsibilities I have?

I'm sure you can add to this list.

These may all be valid conditions, or they may be untrue but we have convinced ourselves they are valid. Before we can really start to have big dreams, we need to understand that most of the time, these conditions are assumptions disguised as truths.

Can you unleash what is inside you without big dreams? I don't think so. Why? Because it's you current level of thinking that got you where you are today. It will not get you where you want to be. Commit to looking, thinking and feeling in a way that may scare you, but it'll only be scary because you will be excited by the new possibilities and afraid of how you will cope if your huge dreams all come crashing down.

In my time working as a coach, I have had numerous clients who stop just sort of their dreams. It's a strange one, this. It's as if they feel at a subconscious level that going for everything they want will mean that if they fail, they will have nowhere else to go. By holding something in reserve, if they do fail, they can still believe they have more to give. This is a false economy for a few reasons:

- They will never know what is really possible for them

- They never actually fail, they just find another way of not allowing their dreams to come true

- They are basically saying to themselves that they don't wholly believe in themselves

List all the conditions that are preventing you from pursuing bigger dreams than you currently have. Are they made up in your head or actually true? Most will likely be made up.

Take something tangible like money, for example. You may not have enough money now to achieve all the things you want to do, but it costs nothing to dream. The cool thing about having big dreams is that you will start to see possibilities everywhere. When this happens, your behaviour, feelings and thoughts adapt, and people around you will notice this. It's a circular thing. Big dreams allow things to happen, and when things happen your dreams will get even bigger.

37. SPEAK AT SCHOOLS

One of the first things I did when I started my entrepreneurial journey was to work in schools, coaching head teachers. With my background in teaching, it was a natural thing to do with my coaching business. One of the offshoots of this was that I was asked to talk to the students.

At first, I said, 'Yeah, OK, that would be fun.' As part of my coaching, I wanted to speak in public more often, but I had never thought about speaking in schools.

The first time I did it was a surreal experience. The great thing about schoolkids is that they are truthful.

They won't hold back and they will ask questions. As part of my own development, speaking in schools taught me a lot about getting to the point, being relevant and making sure I stayed authentic.

There is something about speaking to a group of young people that makes you feel exposed. They couldn't care less about bravado, tactics and strategy. They listen to what you say and immediately notice if it's not real. Irrespective of what you love to do, whether you run your own business, have a job, or practise an art form, find the time to speak in schools. This could be for ten minutes during an assembly, as part of a lesson in class, or as a specially scheduled hour-long talk on your life. Schools are always looking for influential and interesting people to talk to their students. They are not looking for professional speakers; they are looking for people who can give the students an insight into what is possible beyond school.

Don't make speaking in schools a big deal. The first thing to do is to speak to a friend, if you know someone who works in a school. At the very least, you're likely to know someone who knows someone who works in a school. Ask them how to make it happen.

A lot of schools have enterprise days where they look for 'mentors' to come in and assist with the activities. If you become known by your local schools, it will give you an opportunity to be added to their 'banks' of speakers or mentors for such days.

Speaking in schools will build your confidence in presenting. When you can speak in front of school-children, you will be able to speak in front of any audience.

Now we have our mindset in the right place and our game plan worked out, it's time to put it all into action.

PILLAR THREE

THE OUTER GAME

Get Set For Success

38. MODEL SUCCESS

We often look at things like mindset, attitude, talent, and skills as indicators of how successful we may be. But the key ingredient which determines our success is the people we associate with in our environment.

Think about planting a seed. You can have the best seed in the world, but if you put it in the wrong environment, an environment where there is little water, the soil is poor, and the seed has no sunlight, it will not grow. It is no different for human beings.

As humans, we flourish when we are in groups of people who are either likeminded or have higher standards and expectations than we do. Not having these groups around us will stifle our creativity, reduce our confidence and stunt our growth.

Remember when you were at school? If you hung around with a group of people who didn't have high standards, were disruptive, and didn't pay attention in lessons, that group would not have aided your growth, however willing you may have been to grow as a student. But if the people around you had higher expectations and standards than you, they would have helped you to up your game, irrespective of where you mindset was.

If you are at a stage where you want changes in your life, look at the people who you associate with most. Do they inspire you? Do they push you to a new level? If they knew you were looking to make big changes, would they be encouraging or downbeat?

Find a set of people who think like you, want the same things as you and have a positive perspective on life. People with high standards and expectations will be having different conversations and taking different actions, which will naturally influence the kind of actions you will take. Your environment dictates your performance, so choose the people you hang around with carefully.

39. TAKE CALCULATED RISKS

Nothing great occurs without some element of risk.

As you are reading this book, the odds are that you fall into one of the following categories:

- You are stuck in a rut, either in a job you don't like or at a stage in your life where things seem to be stagnant

- You are in between careers and are at crossroads in your life, weighing up what to do next

- You run your own business, it's all very exciting, and you want to make an impact in your industry

- You run your own business and things are OK, but you don't feel excited about things and you want to make some changes

Whatever your situation, you have to take some risks to get different outcomes.

Too many people find themselves in a situation where they've settled for what they have. They come up with reasons why it's either too hard or too uncertain to take the next step. Even though they want to take this step, they feel the risks involved are too much to consider.

There are two universal truths you need to be aware of when we talk about risk: there are no guarantees in life, and change is constant. Because there are no guarantees, calculated risks are necessary for you to feel alive and change the game. And because change is constant, if there is something you want from life, you may as well go for it. Take the risk, as the biggest risk of all is not taking one.

A perception that risk is bad, risk is irresponsible, tends to prevail in life, but the fact is *nothing* can be gained without risk. The question here is not whether you will take risks, but how risky you want to be. That is why the risks we need to take are calculated.

CASE STUDY – GROW CREATIVE COMPANY

Rich With and Michael Shelley founded the Grow Creative Company in 2013. Before that, Rich and Mike were running their own businesses, Rich a design agency and Mike a website development agency. Both were doing really well.

Mike approach Rich with the idea of bringing their individual skillsets together to create a uniquely placed creative agency. They would have the edge that designers like to give their customers along with the skills to create websites with a robust backend support. Both wanted to play a bigger game and offer something different to the market, so they took a calculated risk and Grow Creative Company was born.

On the surface, this may not seem like a high risk. But both men were leaving successful businesses, being their own bosses, answering to no one, having few overheads and no staff costs.

I worked with them to clarify the negotiables: the type of agency they wanted to create and how they were going to be different to other agencies. I'm proud to say that I have been working with Grow Creative Company since its inception, and Rich and Mike have being doing all my branding and website work.

You can check them out here: www.JustGrow.co

In 2005, when I was contemplating leaving my well-paid, ticked-all-the-boxes sales director's job to pursue the dream of starting my own coaching and training business, I had to weigh up how I would provide for my three children and pay the mortgage. A lot of the reasons that had stopped me before were centred around a fear that I wouldn't be able to make it work and be successful. Wasn't I being foolish for contemplating leaving a well-paid job that was giving me everything I needed except satisfaction?

The bottom line was that if I could cover my financial expenses, the risk would be worth taking. Having this clarity made the decision simple. The following year I got my finances in order so I could leave my job on my terms and start my business knowing I had my living costs covered for the next six months.

But what would have happened if the business hadn't worked in those six months? Well, it did, and part of the reason it did was because I had no choice but to make it work. I wasn't going to go back to my unfulfilling job.

When we take a risk and we have our backs against the wall, it is amazing how we find an energy and potential within us that we never knew existed. We all have so much potential in us, but most of us never realise it because we don't take small calculated risks.

If you want to change the game, you have to take risks. There is no other way. It is just not possible to change the game without risks. And what is the worst that could happen? You fail and make a mistake. Invariably you will learn from that mistake and go again with renewed wisdom.

There are so many benefits when you take risks, whether they are related to changing jobs, starting a business, relationships or life decisions.

1. Your self-confidence increases. When you take a risk, you discover something about yourself that you wouldn't have known if you hadn't taken that risk.

2. You overcome the fear of failure. Taking a risk means you break through a fear. When you break through a fear, you realise that it was nowhere near as scary as you expected it to be.

3. You become more creative. Taking a risk, you have to become more creative, whether it is to do with ideas, money or working with others. You think and do things in a different way.

4. You create more opportunities. When you take a risk that gives you new perspectives, opportunities become apparent to you.

5. You stand out. People, both strangers and those close to you, will notice you. They will admire the courage you have and will be secretly wishing they could take a risk as well.

6. You actually achieve your dreams. Many of us have dreams, very few of us realise them. The ones who do take risks. They don't die never knowing what they could have achieved.

7. You learn to trust the process. There are some universal laws, and one of those is that the people who dare are rewarded. Trust that when you follow your heart and dreams, you will get what you want. It may not be exactly as you anticipated, but that's the exciting part.

If you are prepared to do something different and take action that looks risky, do it with a pragmatic mindset. This is about taking calculated risks, not being gung-ho about it. Being gung-ho will lead to loss of confidence, increased fear, and your dreams will remain just dreams. Therefore:

- Don't let emotions dictate your decision making

- Make a plan of action

- Get a mentor – they will keep you on track and be your guide

- Know the worst-case scenario

- Take a small action every day (see Chapter 56, Micro Goals)

Speak to someone you trust about the risk you intend to take. Preferably not a family member or close friend, because they will just want to protect you; you need someone who is going to support you and encourage you and be there whether things work or nor. Speak to someone who gets you and won't pop your bubble. By speaking to someone and getting their support whatever the outcome, you will gain the confidence to take the action.

Now just f***ing do it!

40. ATTEND SEMINARS AND WORKSHOPS

If you study anybody who is successful, whether it is in business, sport, politics, science, or community, they will have invested in themselves. How can you start doing this? My advice would be to attend seminars and workshops.

In 2005, I started thinking about my own life and what I really wanted to do. I was in a good job, but felt empty. It was up to me to change the situation. I realised that if I was to fulfil my dreams and unleash my entrepreneurial spirit, I had to surround myself with different people.

I looked at seminars, workshops and networking events to attend to learn different things on personal development, business, and entrepreneurship. Some were paid events, some were free. Some had thousands of people attending, some had hundreds, some fewer than that.

Attending these events was the start of me really understanding that there were more people than I'd thought who wanted the same kind of things that I wanted from life. They understood me. They were people who didn't accept life as it was: going to school, going to college, either going to university or getting a job, earning enough to buy a house... I'm sure you get the idea. There is no room in this plan for living your dream, creating a life on purpose, or unleashing your entrepreneurial spirit.

Surround yourself with people who up your standard. Attend events at the weekends and in the evenings if you are in full-time work. Networking events have moved on so much in the last few years. They are not just about selling your services and products;

they are about who you are and who you want to become.

When you attend seminars and workshops, several things happen.

1. Your mind expands. Both the subject matter of the seminar and the other people there will teach you something new. The attendees will all have a similar desire to grow and make something of their lives, so it will be easy to make new friends and expand your circle of likeminded people.

2. You see the world differently. When you have a routine of seeing the same people and getting your insights into the world from the same places, for example newspapers, the internet, and TV, your perspective is unlikely to change. Meeting new people outside your normal circle of friends, family and work colleagues will expose you to different views on life.

3. Your wisdom expands. The more you learn, the more you realise there is that you don't know. We get layered with things that we think we need to live, but when we expand our horizons, we see that there is so much more to life than our seven-day work/life routine.

You Are Your Greatest Asset

41. LOOK AFTER YOURSELF

When we think about our most valuable asset, it is amazing how many of us do not invest in it. To clarify, your most valuable asset is *you*. You are born with nothing, and when you die, you can't take anything with you, so investing in yourself will be the best investment you can make.

Changing your game is not about improving one part of your life and ignoring the others. Many stresses and ills come about in our lives because we don't have balance. If we have a good work life, our personal life may be suffering. If we have a good personal life, our work life may be challenging.

You may be one of the lucky few who already has great balance in their life. I would bet that if you are, you are doing at least five of the seven things I have listed in this section.

Investing in yourself is not about becoming a monk and leading a boring life; it's about making consistent changes to ensure that when you need to perform, you are at you best.

Energy is what you need to perform. But I am not talking about drinking energy drinks or caffeine; this is about developing a lifestyle. There are seven things we need to do regularly to ensure we have the energy we require.

1. Eat well. We are what we eat. From personal experience and from speaking to others, I have gathered together some advice to make sure that what you eat will help you be the best version of you.

Gone are the days when it was macho not to eat breakfast because you were too busy. If you skip breakfast, you will get hungry mid-morning, and that's when you'll tend to grab something sugary and unhealthy on the go to give you a badly needed energy boost. The problem will be that you will then have an energy drop later in the day.

'Eat food, not too much, mostly plants.'
— *Michael Pollan, author of various books including* Cooked, Food Rules, *and* In Defense of Food

Michael Pollan advocates a simple philosophy. Eat real food that is unprocessed and doesn't come from a factory. Not too much – this is about portion size. Pollan recommends eating plenty of wholegrain and protein to help you feel satisfied with small portions. Mostly plants – you don't have to become vegetarian or vegan unless you want to, but do make sure you eat plenty of vegetables and fruit.

Eating like this will give you more energy. Try it and see.

2. Sleep well. Sleep deprivation has been associated with heart disease, diabetes and obesity, so it is essential we get the right amount of sleep. See more in Tip 43.

3. Drink plenty of water. The human body is around 60% water. We need water. Lots of it. Men need around 3.5–4 litres a day and women around 2.7 litres a day.

If you drink the recommended amount of water, it helps keep your body fluids in balance. This means you absorb your nutrients better, which will make you feel more energetic. It also helps your skin look better. You concentrate on tasks better when you are hydrated. When you exercise, if you are drinking enough water, you will perform much better. Finally, you will put on less weight because you will eat less if you are full of water.

Drink more water and change your game.

4. Exercise. When we move, we increase our energy, we feel less lethargic, we get healthier, and we perform better. See more in Tip 42.

5. Meditate. Most people are aware of the benefits of eating well, sleeping well, drinking more water and exercising, but still not sure of the real benefits of meditation.

The common misconception is that there is a right way and a wrong way to meditate. This is not true. All meditation means in its most basic form is focusing on one thing. There are more advanced types of meditation where you focus on more than one thing, but for the purpose of this book, I will highlight the benefits of the simple type.

We live in a busy world where everyone and everything wants our attention. To take some time during the day to focus on just one thing can be so good for us. In a nutshell, it slows the beta waves down. Beta waves are all about processing information. When we meditate, we process less information.

This slowing down of the beta waves for twenty to thirty minutes a day helps us with concentration for the rest of the day. We are better focused, less anxious, more creative, and our memory gets better.

6. Read more. Well, you are reading a book now, so that's a good start.

When I say read in this context, I mean read self-help books or autobiographies. When you read, you get to understand other people's viewpoints. Autobiographies are a great way to see what other people have gone through to be a success.

Successful people read a lot. If you don't like reading or just haven't got the time, you can listen to audiobooks while doing something else that's essential to your day like driving, walking or exercising – a win-win all around. Listening to books is a great way to digest information, and with a number of audiobook platforms available nowadays, there is no excuse not to. Personally, I love Audible.

The most successful entrepreneurs read the same books over and over again. When you read a book once, some things will stick more than others, but you cannot take in everything. When you read a book several times, you start to unleash your creative juices. You will see beyond the words to the deeper meaning the author is trying to convey.

There are a couple of books that I have read several times. One is called *The Corporate Mystic* by Gay Hendricks and Kate Ludeman, and the other is *Start With Why* by Simon Sinek. When I read *Start With Why* the first time, it made logical and emotional sense to me. Reading *Start With Why* a second and third time, I became more creative and expansive with my ideas.

Make a list of five of your favourite non-fiction books and commit to reading them again at least one more time.

There is so much creativity within us, but sometimes we need little nudges from the outside world to bring it out. Reading or listening to other people's thoughts and insights can release this creativity and give us new perspectives. Someone else's take on the world can be the very thing we need to bring out our take on it.

7. Meet people. We humans are social animals. All the social media will not replace meeting someone in the flesh. When we physically meet the right people, it can increase our energy levels.

You can take all the action, have the best strategy, have a great purpose, but if you do not invest in yourself then you will be running on empty. Look after yourself and everything will become so much easier because you will have more energy than you know what to do with.

With all these seven things: eating well, sleeping, drinking enough water, exercising, meditating, reading and meeting people, you have to be consistent and persistent to reap the benefits. If you eat well already, that's fine; if not, try it for six weeks and see for yourself the difference it will make to your wellbeing. If you sleep well, great. Otherwise, change your routine and you will see a difference in three to four days.

Drink more water, and within five days, apart from peeing more, you will feel so much better. For exercise, two weeks of consistent action will see a massive difference. If you don't meditate already, this will probably be the most difficult tip to keep on course. But if you do, you will see the most benefit, as this will have a direct impact on the other tips. Audible is a great tool, so it is easier to read more now than it has ever been before. And as for meeting people – well, if you don't meet people, it will be very difficult to change your game. Simple as that.

42. EXERCISE

Most people who don't exercise believe it isn't much fun and feels like hard work. The key here is to find an activity that you enjoy. I am not talking about getting ripped in a gym or exercising seven days a week. Run, walk, cycle, swim, practise a sport – it doesn't matter what it is. As long as you move more than three to four times a week, your energy levels will increase and you will feel much better. There are plenty of books, blogs, and YouTube videos on why it's good to exercise and what you could do.

Without your health, anything else will be fruitless. To be at your best, to have the energy to live your entrepreneurial spirit, you have to be healthy.

Here are some of the benefits of regular exercise:

- It keeps your energy up
- You feel motivated
- You will keep your weight down
- It reduces the risk of heart disease
- It reduces stress
- It boosts brainpower
- You have more energy and can get more done
- It increases creativity
- It sharpens memories
- It improves self-confidence

Don't ignore the benefits of being physically healthy. A lot of the tips in this book work on your mind. Keep the body healthy as well.

A point of caution here: if you already do regular exercise, that's great. If you don't, don't put too much pressure on yourself by setting high goals. Start with small exercise sessions and build up as your fitness improves.

Get moving and get motivated.

43. SLEEP

There is a common misconception that entrepreneurs constantly burn both ends of the candle and only sleep for a couple of hours a night. But that is not true. We entrepreneurs know as well as anyone that when we get enough sleep, we are better during the day.

You need to know how much sleep you need. For some people, that will eight hours a night; others can get by on as little as four to five hours.

These are some indicators that you are not getting enough sleep:

- Your emotions are all over the place
- You get ill regularly
- You are always hungry
- You put on weight

- You are more impulsive

- You forget things

- You have trouble making decisions

There are some simple things you can do to sleep better:

- Develop a relaxed bedtime routine

- Switch off all your electronic gadgets and wind down for an hour before you sleep

- Watch what you eat and drink before bedtime

There will always be extreme exceptions. To achieve anything good in your life, you have to put the work in, so there will be times when you will have to work sixteen- to eighteen-hour days. But make sure these are not the norm.

Are you a morning person or an evening person? When are you at your most productive? I could show you 1,000 successful people who wake up at 5am every day and are more productive between the hours of 5am and 9am than most people are between 9am and 5pm. These people know that whatever happens for the rest of the day, they have already got a lot done. It's in the bank.

Would this routine work for you? Or would you perform better waking up at 7.30am, getting productive from around 9.30am, and then splitting your day up between tasks, and maybe working for a few hours in the evening too? Perhaps you do your best work after 7pm, so could you work until midnight? Again, I could show you 1,000 people who are highly successful with a routine like this.

There is no right or wrong routine, so find the one that works for you. Whatever routine you choose, though, it is vital that you get the right amount of quality sleep. Sleep is essential for good health, and without your health, you achieve nothing.

Sleep allows our brain to function. We know this because we can see the negative impact on the brain's function when we don't get enough sleep. Without enough sleep, the part of the brain that controls our language, memory, planning and sense of time will become severely affected. The brain practically shuts down.

Lack of sleep also impacts our emotional and physical health. When we don't sleep enough, we are more likely to gain weight, have high blood pressure and be at a higher risk of diabetes and heart attacks. Lack of sleep affects our response mechanisms and our ability to think clearly and be creative.

Gone are the days when the attitude was that sleep is for losers and those not hungry for success. Look after yourself first rather than driving for success at any cost.

What can you do to ensure you get quality sleep?

Create a sleep schedule. You will likely know how much sleep you need to function properly during the day. Typically it will be between seven and nine hours. If you like to wake early and get things done, then ensure you are in bed in time to get your seven to nine hours.

There are many apps available that will help you analyse and optimise your sleep patterns.

Turn off technology. Over-exposure to the blue light emitted by electronic devices has been proven to disrupt sleep patterns, so make sure your phone, tablet, TV etc are all turned off at least an hour before bedtime.

Take power naps. Factor in a mid-afternoon nap if you can. This only needs to be for ten to fifteen minutes to reset you for the rest of the day.

44. TAKE HOLIDAYS

When we're planning our business, we need to plan out what to achieve so we can have a life we want, whether that is a life of free time, travelling, or feeding our soul. Taking time for ourselves is essential, but we often only tend to do this when all the other stuff relating to our business has been looked after.

Some may say that when we do what we love and we love what we do, it doesn't feel like work, so why would we need a holiday? As humans, we *all* need to take time out to rest our bodies and minds, however much we may love the work we do. Taking holidays is as important as the time we spend on our career or business, if not more so in some cases.

Holidays should not be a nice to have, but a necessity. We will only achieve what we want and change the way we play the game if we allow ourselves time out to recharge and relax.

Although it will take hard work and commitment to change your game, don't forget the importance of investing in yourself. A healthy entrepreneur is a successful entrepreneur.

Getting Started

45. TAKE MASSIVE ACTION AND HUSTLE

The word 'hustle' can have negative connotations. To some, it implies that a person is a bit shady, a fraud without consideration for others. But in terms of the context in which I am using it here, 'hustle' refers to making things happen when they seem impossible. Hustling is about asking anyway, even when the odds are against you; calling someone expecting them to say no; committing to something when you know it requires you to step outside your comfort zone; doing something that goes against the grain of logic.

The game cannot change without you taking massive action, and hustling is all part of that.

It may not seem it, but by reading this book, you are taking massive action. This book may be the first you have read that talks to your heart in a way that no other book has. Or it may be one of several books you have read which have done this.

Why hustle? Why take massive action? Why must you never give up? Because life is not fair. Luck will come your way when you understand that everything you want is available to you, but only if you are prepared to do what most people are not even prepared to think about.

The hustle starts in your mind. Choose that you will accept nothing less than your standards require. When you concede that, be prepared for everything to conspire against you. Your fear will want to convince you that you're not good enough, it's the wrong time, it's too late, you're too old, too young, you don't have enough experience. Whatever excuses your fear can think of will show up and imposter syndrome will kick in with a vengeance. That's why taking massive action before the doubts kick in is essential, so hustle persistently and don't take no for an answer.

Changing the game in your life brings great rewards, but these rewards come with sacrifice. All the suggestions in the book require some sort of sacrifice, so if you are going to take action, it may as well be big, hairy-arsed action. The people who are making waves in the marketplace have done exactly that at some point. For some, massive action is all they know.

Be prepared for failure. In fact, if you don't fail, you are not taking big enough actions or hustling hard enough. Failure is the indicator that you are taking the action you need, so don't fall at the first hurdle. Hustle; take massive action. The world is waiting for you to change the game.

46. START NOW

If you don't start, you won't get anywhere. People often talk about when they will start, but they never actually do it. They wait until they believe everything is in place, the conditions are right, they have learnt a new skill, they have gained more experience. Some people even wait for the weather to be right! The problem with all this is that there is never a right time to start. The only time you can start is now.

Let me tell you a little secret: the fact that you are reading this book means you have already started. The key thing to realise, though, is that once you have started changing the game intellectually, you need to follow through by taking appropriate action. The good news is that most of the actions you need to take are quite small and manageable. You will only feel overwhelmed if you go for the big picture right from the start and realise the enormity of what you are trying to create. Concentrate on the micro actions you can take right now and know you are on your way to achieving your big dream.

Apple, Walt Disney, Harley Davidson, Hewlett Packard, Mattel, and Microsoft – what do they all have in common? They all started in a garage. But many people look at these large, successful organisations and think, *Wow! If I had their resources, I would be able to create something massive.* What they don't realise is where most of these organisations started. All they had was a garage and an idea.

> 'It's not about resources; it's about your resourcefulness.'
> — *Tony Robbins*

When you are thinking about taking action towards your dream, what's stopping you? Is it some internal fear? The fear of doing something wrong? The fear of not looking great? Or do you honestly believe you do not have the skills yet to execute what you want to do? I would suggest that all of these excuses are either not true, or easier to address than you may think. Visit www.EnSpirit.Global to find resources that will complement the advice in this book and help you start the projects and adventures you want.

Before you take any of the actions I've listed below, connect once again with your why. For example, if you want to lose weight, concentrate on why that is.

Do you want to look great in your clothes? Feel more healthy? Run marathons? If you want to make more money, concentrate on why you want the money. Is it for a specific lifestyle? A house by the sea? Your kids' education? Look beyond the action you want to take to the reason you want to take it.

Once you have your why in the centre of your mind, start taking action towards your goal.

Accountability. Your first task is to find someone who will hold you accountable. Ideally this will be a coach, mentor or group of people who understand your why and challenge you. Do not choose family and friends; although they may understand what you want to achieve, they are likely to allow you to get away with not following through. A coach, mentor or group of people who are doing similar things to you will not allow this.

Journal. We can't always appreciate what we have already achieved, all the little actions that have an impact on the bigger picture. Keeping a daily journal of what you have and have not done will be a great way of keeping track, and more importantly, it will keep you motivated to achieve your goals. Have a look at www.EnSpirit.Global where you will find a way to create your own journal.

Join the EnSpirit Facebook group. In this private group, you will find likeminded, motivated people who want more from their lives. You can request to join here: www.facebook.com/groups/EnSpirit

47. FIND A COACH/MENTOR

There will be times in your life when you will believe you know what to do. Everything you need will be at your disposal, but you won't take action. Or if you do take action, you won't get the desired results. Something will not be right.

Years back, coaching was introduced into workplaces to solve toxic issues with people or cultures that were not performing. Now, coaching is used much more proactively to develop highly performing people. Coaching, when used in the right way, is all about sharpening the sword. Elite sportspeople have always used coaches in this way, because coaches bring out the best in them. Coaches see things that people don't see in themselves, and they ask questions that get people to think in a different way.

If you research top businesspeople like Richard Branson, Steve Jobs, Elon Musk, they have all used a coach in some capacity. And a lot of the tips in this book will be much easier to achieve if you're working with a coach. A good coach allows you to get out of your own way and become highly productive.

CASE STUDY – WILL POLSTON

If you google Will Polston, you will see he is a mindset strategist who runs the Elite Network. This network offers online courses and a number of business and personal development workshops. Will knows his stuff, he makes things happen, and he is fully focused.

When Will contacted me to ask if I would work with him, I said I would love to. This may surprise you – why would a coach who is making waves in the world need a coach? The answer is so he can make even bigger waves. Will wants the edge, and through the coaching we did together, he is upping his game all the time.

Will told me that he chose to work with me because my values are aligned with his, and this is an important consideration when you're choosing a coach or mentor. He regarded me as more than a mentor, appreciating my academic understanding of coaching and psychology, too.

Get a coach who is right for you, to give you the edge you want.

Here I want to highlight ten things a good coach can offer to help you change your game.

1. Understanding. A coach or mentor will help you understand yourself better.

We all have default excuses to justify why we don't do things, but a coach won't allow you these excuses.

They will clarify your end goals and ask questions to discover actions that work towards your goals.

2. Emotional support. We are human beings, not machines. A good coach will understand your emotional triggers and help you through periods of low self-esteem, self-doubt and low confidence.

When you make a decision to live life on your terms, often the people closest to you will have trouble adjusting to the new you. Having to justify the things you do and why you are doing them can become tiring and lonely, so a good coach will support you to stay on course with empathy and encouragement.

3. Specific core skills. As well as asking you the right questions at the right time, a good coach will also teach you a lot. Looking from the outside in, they are not emotionally involved with your decision making. Emotions can cloud your judgement, so a coach helps you to develop your communication skills, team-building skills and effective delegation. These are core skills for entrepreneurs.

4. Confidence. One of the primary reasons someone works with a coach is to take action to grow faster as a person. Coaches ensure you follow up on tasks and keep to deadlines, which has a side benefit: your confidence will grow.

In the personal development world, some people presume that you need to be confident before you take action, but it is often the other way round. Taking action leads to increased confidence. A good coach gives you the environment to take the right action as well as the scope to fail, because this is when your greatest growth happens. A coach by your side will ensure you learn from failure quickly and go again with increased knowledge and confidence.

5. Purpose. When you decide to change your game, you are really deciding to live your life on purpose. When you work with a coach who knows your why, they will help you stay on course.

The minutiae of life can put you back and decrease your confidence when you are not getting the day-to-day results you want. A coach makes a stand for you to keep on purpose.

6. Leaning in. When things get tough, our human instinct is to back away and either think about it or resist getting uncomfortable. When we lean in to a problem or obstacle, we are forced to face our fears and work through them.

The only agenda a good coach has for you is to be and perform at your best, to be highly productive and to go beyond what you believe is possible. Leaning in is the difference between the people who do and the people who don't make it in life.

7. Blind spot recognition. There are things you know you know, and there are things you know you don't know, and there are things you don't know you don't know. These last things are your blind spots. A good coach will help you to identify your blind spots.

We all have blind spots, but we can't deal with something we can't see. A coach will be our mirror.

8. Honesty. A good coach will be honest with you. When things are good, they will tell you. When things are not going well, they will tell you. When you are not stepping up, they will tell you. When you have performed beyond your limits, they will tell you.

Living life on your own terms will have its challenges, so you need someone around you who will tell you the truth. Sometimes it will be uncomfortable, but the safety net of having a coach who has your best interests at heart can be the most powerful tool in your armoury.

9. Power. A coach or mentor does not 'teach' you stuff; they see more potential in you than you see in yourself. They ask questions that get you to think from a different perspective. If you think of the number of things you have to deal with in life and work, the decisions and actions you have to take, they can sometimes overwhelm you. The insights and perspective of someone else can therefore be incredibly empowering.

> 'We ask ourselves, who am I to be brilliant, gorgeous, talented, and fabulous? Actually, who are you not to be?'
> — *Marianne Williamson, author and spiritual teacher*

We don't always know how powerful we are. We cannot see how much potential we have, but a good coach can and they will help us to recognise the power we all have within.

10. A break from the internal chatter. When you work with someone whose sole responsibility is to ensure you operate and perform at your best, your internal chatter quietens down. You will stop procrastinating over things that don't matter and just get on with it.

Coaching is conceptual, so to understand the power of it, you need to experience it. Coaching will challenge you to go beyond what you think you are capable of, meaning your self-imposed limits will be shattered and you will think of the world in a different way. Assumptions kill your creativity and decision-making skills. A good coach/mentor will create the environment for you to explore a world where you don't have these assumptions and can make different choices to take different actions.

When you're choosing a coach or mentor, speak to a few to get a feel for which one will be right for you. Each coach has his or her own style, so google them, see what the world says about them, what experience they have. Speak to people who have used them before and get an idea of how they work. Network at events and see how coaches operate. Many coaches speak in public, so go and see what you like about them.

Another thing you need to do when you're contemplating finding a coach is to make sure you are coachable. Don't be closed to anything they may suggest.

Make a list of all the things you want from a coach or mentor, then find someone trustworthy who will challenge you and not be afraid to tell you the truth. Of all the tips in this book, in my opinion, finding the perfect coach or mentor is probably the most important.

48. LOOK FOR OPPORTUNITIES THAT CHALLENGE YOU

What does success look like to you? What do you see below?

Opportunityisnowhere

You will either see opportunity is nowhere or opportunity is now here. Depending on your point of view, you will see opportunity either everywhere you look, or never crossing your path.

Those who change the game don't wait for opportunities to come to them; they make opportunities happen. More importantly, they create opportunities that challenge them.

There is no point taking or creating an opportunity that does not challenge you. Nothing exciting happens within your current comfort zone. One of the best books to get you thinking about how to create opportunities that challenge you is *The Big Leap* by Gay Hendricks. In this book, Gay talks about the four different zones that we operate in.

Zone of incompetence. This is where we do something we are not good at and we know other people can do it better. It's best to avoid these tasks altogether.

Zone of competence. We can do a task perfectly well, but so can others. By delegating these tasks, we can free up time for tasks that really excite us.

Zone of excellence. This is where we do things really well. We are comfortable here, but we know deep inside that we are capable of much more.

Zone of genius. This is where the real fun is. Performing in this zone means we are living a fully satisfied life. In this zone, we are truly challenged.

Most of us operate between the zone of competence and the zone of excellence, depending on what environment and circumstances dictate. This is understandable if we think about it. Why would we deliberately put ourselves in a situation where we are uncomfortable?

But to get what we really want from our life, we have to push our limits.

When we only operate from our zone of competence, we settle, we sell out, we give up on life. Game changers don't do that. Changing the game means you have to challenge yourself. When you challenge yourself, you will see opportunities that really excite you.

To find out more, I thoroughly recommend you read *The Big Leap.*

When we operate from our zone of genius, there is no hiding place. So how do we operate from this zone and seek new opportunities?

Be curious. Accept nothing as it is. Don't assume anything and don't think something can't be done another way. How could you approach the issues from a completely different standpoint?

We are born curious. Watch children – they don't accept anything; they explore and discover. Operate from the point of view of your inner child to see what is possible.

Meet new people. We attract and associate with people like ourselves. To really push yourself, you need to meet people from different backgrounds with different interests and different life experiences.

Read things that you wouldn't normally read. Challenge yourself to read about stuff you may not agree with, or even stuff you think you have no interest in. You never know what lightbulbs will be triggered.

Observe people and things. Look. I mean really look and pay attention to the world. See how other people operate, how they think, and what they do. Look at how things happen. What patterns occur in the world? What pattern can you break? If you see how to do something differently, you start to operate from your zone of genius.

Travel. When you travel, you experience different cultures and meet more of the 7.5 billion people on the planet. They will ask you different questions, they will see you in a different way, and they will help you to see yourself in a different light.

Pick one of these five things and do it today. Take action and see how your life changes when new opportunities fall into your lap.

49. BE CONSISTENT

'It's not what we do once in a while that shapes our
lives. It's what we do consistently.'
— *Tony Robbins*

If you want to know the secret sauce of success, the
one thing that separates the great, the highly successful, the ultra-achievers from everyone else, it's being
consistent. Consistency is the sauce that will keep you
in the game; consistency is the sauce that will separate you from the ordinary; consistency is the sauce
that will make the difference. It's not difficult to be
consistent, but as humans, we are often inherently
lazy. We want an easy ride.

What does it require to be consistent? It takes being
completely committed. It takes an unquestionable passion for something. It takes being focused without dis-
traction. Consistency starts with you making a choice
to aim for what you believe in and not wavering from
that. It is a long-term commitment. It's about creating
good habits. It's about keeping going when you don't
feel like doing it. It's sticking to the things you have to
do to get what you want without making excuses.

There is no free lunch in life; you get what you work
for, and you get luckier the more work you put in.
The most successful people do not focus on the short
term. Yes, they break things down and have daily
habits that ensure small gains, but all these small

gains work towards the big objective. Successful people don't settle for short-term gratification and rest on their laurels.

An Olympic athlete works towards a tournament which only happens once every four years. That is a long time to wait for their ultimate reward. But in order for them to be ready to win gold, they have to have been super consistent in their training over those four years. Any lapse in consistency will result in them taking two steps forward and two steps back.

Being inconsistent will mean you are always playing catch-up with yourself, but there is a cost to being consistent. That cost is that you actively evolve. Being consistent means you have to have habits and repetition, but it also requires you to evolve in your learning, thinking and awareness.

Being consistent also requires you to be fully present and avoid any distractions. Any successful undertaking requires mindful consistency. The struggle many people have with commitment is that they need instant gratification. This need occurs because they have not planned ahead; they have not thought of the overarching reason why they want to be consistent. This overarching reason will come down to their core values and purpose. We live by our core values; these are the anchors of our lives. If one of our core values is health, for example, we won't compromise on keeping fit and eating the right things.

When our actions are aligned with our core values and passions, life is so much easier. The struggle comes when we are inconsistent, which tends to occur when the actions we take are not aligned with our core values. When the action doesn't produce an immediate result, there is no motivation to continue and so we give up.

Be clear on your core values and embrace consistency in your life.

Good Habits

50. WRITE A BOOK

Writing a book has so many benefits, but often people who could do this, don't.

The likelihood is you will fall into one of four categories:

1. You have written a book.

2. You have thought about writing a book and have started.

3. You have thought about writing a book but have not started.

4. You have never thought of writing a book.

We all have something to say; we all have a gift; we all have something that someone else in the world needs. Whatever it is for you that drives you to change your game, writing a book will crystallise it.

The two main excuses people give for not writing a book are 'I don't have anything to say' and 'I don't have time'. Let's deal with the first one. We all have something to say, especially entrepreneurs and game changers. As you are reading this book, I'm guessing you are someone who does have a drive and inner fire waiting to come out. So what is your big message? What do you have to say that would give people an insight they didn't have before? What would tell the world what you stand for? What do you know to be true, but no one else sees it the same way? That will be the subject matter for the book you need to write.

What about the second excuse? You will always find time for the things that mean the most to you, and what could be more important than introducing your passion to the world?

51. ASK QUESTIONS

The more questions you ask, the better your questions will get.

As small children, if we ask too many questions, we are often told to sit down and shut up. In school, if we ask a question that our fellow students think is silly, we get ridiculed. We grow up in a society where we believe we have to act as if we know it all or stay small in our own world. As a result, we tend to stop asking questions.

The tragic thing about this is that the best way to grow and be entrepreneurial is to ask questions. Lots of questions. When you ask questions, you show that you have a growth mindset. Questions have the power to unleash your creative potential. Developing your entrepreneurial spirit is about being more creative, because being creative develops new ideas, which lead to innovations, which make the world a better place. And all because you asked more questions.

If the Wright brothers hadn't asked questions, we wouldn't have planes. If Martin Luther King hadn't asked questions, we would still live in a divided society. If Alexander Bell hadn't asked questions, we wouldn't have the telephone. If I hadn't asked questions back in 2005, you wouldn't be reading this book now.

Asking questions can get you the life you want, so what questions are you not asking yourself? Or if you are asking questions, maybe you are not giving truthful answers because then you would have to act on them. What questions are you not asking others? Maybe you are asking the questions but not getting the answers you want.

The beauty of questions is that the more you ask, the better your results will be. Stop looking for the answers and start looking for better questions to ask.

52. PRACTISE LIKE IT MATTERS

It's funny how the mind just knows when something matters. When something is really important to you, you get stressed about it, tense up, make it mean more than it does. This is why practising like it matters makes such a difference.

Take this in a sporting context. Practising and training are essential if you are to perform, but there are two forms of practice: practising and training because you have to, and practising and training because the outcome matters to you. You are all in. You practise like you are performing the real thing.

If you run your own business, there will be training you do to update your skills and learn new strategies. When you are doing this training, immerse yourself and really get into it. For example, when you read this book, make notes and read the chapters several times. This is practice for the real thing, for when you implement all that you have learnt.

When you practise like it matters, you engage your body as well as your mind. Your muscles have memory, so when you immerse yourself into something using mind, body and spirit, your muscles will remember it. Then when you are 'in the game', your muscles will remember the practice and react accordingly. The repeated actions you have been practising won't feel strange when it matters. You will feel in flow.

The body doesn't know when something matters and when it doesn't. It can fool the mind and trick it into thinking the activity is just another practice when you are doing it for real, and you will perform naturally and without stress. When you practise to make every moment count, you will also save time when it matters.

Don't just turn up when you think it matters, turn up all the time. You never know what will happen, what opportunities will present themselves, and who may be watching. So many of us spend so much time trying to find shortcuts for whatever we need to do that we forget to get on with it. Yes, it's great to find smart ways to do things, but don't just give your practice lip service. Go all in.

So how do you practise like it matters?

Prepare. This is where routines and rituals are so important. When you have routines and rituals, you set yourself up for what you want to achieve in your day.

Don't focus on the outcome. Yes, have the outcome in mind, but don't focus on achieving it. Focus on how you practise and how you will turn up.

Feel it. You know when you are giving something lip service and when you are playing full out. Feel it and immerse yourself in the experience.

Pick one project in your business or life and create a list of things you need to practise to execute it. Do you need more information? Do you need to speak to others about it? Do you need more resources? Whatever it is, practise like it matters and play to win.

53. GET GOOD AT PRESENTING

We now live in a world where what we stand for or what we say will not cut it on its own. The way we communicate and how we present will have a massive impact on how our message is received.

Social media has levelled the playing field and the entry level for all of us to create content, present and be more visible. This is not to say we all have to become YouTube stars; what it means is that to make the impact we want to make, we have to be able to communicate and present effectively and be comfortable with being more visible.

When you are good at presenting, you ensure that your audience will listen to you and pay attention. If it's hard work for the audience to listen to your presentation, they will switch off.

Being great at presenting means you are seen as an authority. You are noticed and people will seek you out. Video is the new norm. If you are not comfortable on video, get comfortable. Seek out people who are good on video and ask for help. And do the same thing with presenting. Become comfortable with presenting to groups of people.

The good news is this: all you need to be when presenting, either in front of an audience or on video, is yourself. If you need a little confidence boost and some easy techniques to follow when presenting, seek these out and make a change.

54. BE VISIBLE

This is about how you are seen online. If you want to change the game, you have to be visible. The format doesn't matter: written, video, audio, images, or graphics. The most important thing is that people know what you are about before they even meet you.

Social media is part of the DNA of society; you cannot avoid it. What you can do, though, is use it in a way that works for you. Whether you are a professional, run your own business, or have a career, if you want to change the game, you need to be highly visible on social.

I have created a nine-stage framework to show you how you can be more visible and authentic.

Phase 1 – ignite:
1. Audience – identify your audience

2. Listen – listen to what they are saying

3. Acknowledge – recognise them

Phase 2 – engage:
1. Connections – make connections

2. Conversations – talk to your audience

3. Content – create your own content

Phase 3 – influence:
1. Publish – publish your own content

2. Repurpose – cross populate your own content

3. Amplify – spread your message far and wide

This framework gives you a good way to build up your visibility by being about value rather than marketing.

To be visible, you also need to be available. This is not about saying yes to everything; in fact, saying no can be more powerful. What this is about is allowing your viewpoint and your expertise to be easily available to others. You can do this by being active on social, writing a book, publishing blogs, giving interviews, connecting with people at networking events, and being around people you feel slightly uncomfortable with. This all means you have to be on the top of your game.

55. JOIN A MASTERMIND

If I were asked what has made the biggest impact on my development, both personally and business-wise, I would say joining a mastermind group.

The concept of a mastermind group was first developed by Napoleon Hill in his book *The Law of Success* (1920), and revised and expanded in his more famous book *Think and Grow Rich* (1930). By the way, if you haven't read this book, I highly recommend that you do. Napoleon Hill first called it a 'mastermind alliance', but nowadays it is more commonly known as a mastermind group.

> '[A mastermind alliance is] the coordination of
> knowledge and effort of two or more people, who
> work towards a definite purpose, in the spirit of
> harmony. No two minds ever come together without
> thereby creating a third, invisible, intangible force,
> which may be likened to a third mind.'
> — *Napoleon Hill*

When you are part of a mastermind group, you benefit from a third viewpoint that would never have occurred through a simple conversation.

There are some rules to a mastermind group that make it different to group coaching or a mentoring session:

- You must have three or more people – I would recommend you have no more than twelve to make it really effective

- Each member brings an issue/problem/challenge that they would like solutions to

- All members get a fair chance to talk about their issue while the others listen

- The group then has a chance to ask questions to clarify points, but can't give any solutions

- Once this is finished, each member gives a solution from their perspective which the recipient cannot acknowledge; they just take notes

- Once this round is complete, the member with the challenge will give their feedback and what they will do next; the facilitator makes a note of this and the group then holds the challenger accountable to take the action

- This process is repeated for each member

This is the principal of masterminding. The format may vary from group to group, but it is essentially a forum to brainstorm different ideas and get out of your own head to get things done.

When I have been part of masterminding, the impact has been immeasurable. There is no hiding place. No one takes any nonsense. My normal excuses for not getting things done are not tolerated, and I always leave with an action plan that I can implement and will be held accountable for. Another benefit is that invariably, the other people in the group are from different industries, so they don't have the 'baggage' of how my industry works and come from a clean mindset.

There are many groups you could join, so do a search online for mastermind groups. Mostly they charge, but it is a worthwhile investment. Or you could start one yourself. All you need is a group of five to six likeminded people who are willing to be challenged and held accountable to take action in the areas they know will make a difference in their business and life.

If you are reading this book, the odds are you are ready to take massive action. Joining or creating a mastermind group will help you in that.

56. MICRO GOALS

Daily actions are key to changing your game. Setting daily micro goals is key.

Micro goals allow you to take incremental steps each day which give you a sense of achievement. Micro goals are different to normal goals. Usually goals get you to aim for the stars, and if you miss you will hit the moon. Micro goals aim for the moon and hit the moon.

Micro goals have a specific structure.

1. You are in total control. The overall goal could be to close two clients, so the micro goal is to make ten calls. Whatever happens after the tenth call just happens. The micro goal is something you have total control over, unlike the overall goal.

2. They are measurable. You know, I know and the world knows you have achieved your micro goals. For example, a micro goal could be to write 1,000 words for a book every day. It is not to research for the book, which is too open-ended.

3. They can be achieved within two hours. The micro goal should not take up your whole day, but it needs to allow you to move forward, achieve something, and make you feel good. This gives you the energy to do the other things you want to do in the day.

Being consistent with micro goals means you are likely to achieve more in a week than you would ever believe possible.

Well done! You are now familiar with the three pillars of game-changing success. Having got this far, you have already shown a high level of commitment.

Final Thoughts

One of the most common things I get asked is, 'What is the one thing that is the key to success/getting what I want/being happy, etc?' Well, the truth is there isn't one single thing; there isn't one secret sauce. There may be one thing that creates a tipping point, but there is rarely a single thing will bring you success.

When people talk about an overnight success, they don't see the years of hard work that have gone into it. There is no such thing as a free lunch. Taking action without a strategy will only give you short-term success; constantly questioning your thoughts and beliefs without taking action will lead to inertia. You don't have to change yourself; all you need to do is change the game you play.

The rules are universal: think, plan, act. It's not rocket science. The tips in this book will show you how to join up the dots. The work is what you do. But how you turn up for that work has the greatest impact.

It starts with you.

It ends with you.

Make sure the middle part is you at your best.

Acknowledgements

This book would not have been possible without the support of my family. Sangita, Sapna, Milan and Suraj inspire me to be my best.

My extended family for their individual support; many of the insights in the book come from conversations that have nothing to do with entrepreneurship.

My special friends, you know who you are. We have lunch; we speak weekly; we connect on WhatsApp.

My clients: I cannot ignore the support I get from you on social media platforms. Every like, comment, share and heart has inspired me to write this book.

My extended network. I am part of many networks and groups, all of which have three things in common:

1. You don't need to justify yourself

2. The members don't allow you to stay in the cesspit; they pull you up

3. You find out who you truly are

Of the many groups I belong to, I would particularly like to thank BeCollaboration, Key Person of Influence, Landmark, The Yes Group and The Elite Network for their support.

Lucy and Joe and the team at Rethink Press, for all your support with getting this book published.

Thank you all.

The Author

Award-winning businessman and TEDx speaker Baiju Solanki is the CEO/founder of EnSpirit Global: a platform that serves to awaken, instil and enhance the entrepreneurial spirit in all those who wish to live their best life.

A former Businessman of the Year, Baiju has experience which extends beyond the realm of enterprise. A trained psychologist, lecturer, speaker and author, he nudges people into realising their power.

Baiju had experience in the academic world as a psychology lecturer and in the corporate world as a sales director before starting his own coaching and training business in 2007. Using his skills as a trainer, teacher and coach, he aims to transform the world through teaching entrepreneurial skills to businesspeople, start-ups, students and employees to increase productivity, performance and winning mindsets. His mission is to teach people that being an entrepreneur doesn't need to have anything to do with business; it's a mindset centred on making the most of what is available to you now, and thriving.

You can find out more about EnSpirit Global by following these links:

www.EnSpirit.Global
www.twitter.com/EnSpiritGlobal
www.instagram.com/EnSpiritGlobal
www.facebook.com/EnSpiritGlobal
www.linkedin.com/company/EnSpiritGlobal

Or connect with Baiju Solanki at:

www.BaijuSolanki.com
www.twitter.com/BaijuSolanki
www.instagram.com/BaijuSolanki
www.facebook.com/Baiju.Solanki
www.linkedin.com/in/baijusolanki
www.youtube.com/watch?v=HA-TFRXRWPY

Now Your First Action...

Are you going to achieve your potential? Find out here and take the Change Your Game Scorecard:

www.EnSpirit.Global/potentialscorecard.html